TO THE POINT
CONFRONTING YOUTH ISSUES

VIOLENCE

Edited by
Diana L. Hynson

Abingdon Press
Nashville

TO THE POINT
CONFRONTING YOUTH ISSUES

TABLE OF CONTENTS

VIOLENCE

A Word From the Editors

We are faced every day with grim reports and statistics about the effects of violence, even in places that ought to be safe. Violence is not just a problem in housing projects, ghetto streets, or nonwhite population areas. It is not something the middle class can blame on "them" (the ones not like "us"). These stereotypes are just that, incorrect images that neither describe the scope and extent of the problem, nor offer constructive means to confront it.

We Learn What We See

Dr. Deborah Prothrow-Stith, an eminent physician and public educator, says:

"We are a suggestible species. We learn how to behave from each other. When we see one of our species act, their act becomes a model for us to emulate. In this way, we sometimes make the unthinkable thinkable, the undoable doable. We can learn how to kill a president from a movie. We can learn how to commit suicide from each other. We can also learn how to commit mass murder." (From *Deadly Consequences*: *How Violence Is Destroying Our Teenage Population and a Plan to Begin Solving the Problem*, by Deborah Prothrow-Stith, M.D. and Michaele Weissman. Copyright © 1991 by Deborah Prothrow-Stith and Michaele Weissman. Reprinted by permission of HarperCollins Publishers, Inc.)

Publicity is one culprit in this power of suggestion; by bringing the behavior into the spotlight, we provide the opportunity to imitate, even emulate it. It should be no secret by now that children, youth, and adults see huge amounts of violence, from movies; television; toys, like "hero" dolls; and their parents and peers.

Dr. Prothrow-Stith goes on to say:

"Like many psychologists I believe that the family and social environment can teach children to use violence to solve problems . . .

"According to social learning theory, children learn how to behave aggressively by watching others use violence to their advantage and then imitating what they have seen. This process is called 'modeling.' Parents who have seen their three- or four-year-old watch a newcomer at the playground and then later reproduce the newcomer's unpleasant habit—throwing sand at other children, for example—know

how powerful a learning tool modeling is. Modeling is only part of the picture, however. The modeled behavior will become a part of the child's standard repertoire only if it is reinforced." (From *Deadly Consequences*, HarperCollins, 1991; page 44)

Positive behavior is also emulated when it is reinforced, but our children and youth see so much negative behavior that we need a concerted family, church, community, and national effort to counteract the national, pervasive standard of aggression and violence that seems to be the first choice in problem solving. TO THE POINT: *VIOLENCE* is our most recent contribution to the cause.

TO THE POINT: VIOLENCE

Violence comes in many forms. TO THE POINT: *VIOLENCE* addresses some of these, including gang violence, date rape, sexual abuse, dangerous classmates, and ritual abuse. *VIOLENCE* provides teaching articles to prepare adults who work with youth to deal with some of the hard realities of violence and to teach them how to recognize, address, and protect themselves and teens legally. Other articles include "Being Pastoral," "Legal Knowledge Is Key," and "Language and Violence."

Violence is not just a sad and frightening phenomenon of the inner city. It is our heritage, even from the days of Cain and Abel. "Violence in the Bible" helps us understand and make meaning theologically of this unfortunate, but inescapable fact of life.

Our Work for Peace

TO THE POINT: *VIOLENCE* is not the complete or final word on how to cope with violence. It does not provide all the answers on how to live as peacemakers and peacekeepers. But it is a step, an accessible tool for youth and adults who work with them to be in ministry with survivors and perpetrators of violence.

What distinguishes *VIOLENCE* from a social commentary or workbook on violence is its biblical base. Most of the articles and all of the programs provide biblical and theological insight to dealing with different forms of violence, its victims, and its perpetrators. If the church, who claims its identity in the name of the Prince of Peace, is not at the forefront of our confrontation with evil, how shall we stand against it?

Diana L. Hynson
Gail G. Bock

How to Use This Resource

TO THE POINT: *VIOLENCE*

Violence is a crucial subject for teens today. As an adult worker with youth, you may have found yourself hearing conversations around the fringes of youth group activities and conversations. You may be hearing teens talk about fears at school or in other settings, including the home. You may notice someone showing signs of abuse.

You realize that there are numerous resources on the market and you need to find a choice that allows you a variety of approaches to the subject. You know you need to be able to talk to teens from a biblical and theological context too. Wanting to help is just not enough. This issue of **TO THE POINT** will provide background and references to assist you in this crucial caring ministry.

TO THE POINT: *VIOLENCE*
Offers Ready-Made Programs

If you want to offer a program or series of programs in the youth fellowship setting, in a retreat, or other organized class, the "Programs" section is the place to begin. Each program gives you about forty minutes of discussion, activities, games, and other options for an organized learning setting. The teaching articles can easily be adapted for formal settings as well. And the program ideas offer added helps for how to begin and sustain a discussion and other hints.

TO THE POINT: *VIOLENCE*
Helps You Help Others

Perhaps one of the most poignant and difficult tasks for you, as an adult friend to teens, is how to help them when they are hurting, frightened, confused, or angry. The section "When Someone Comes to You" will help you get a handle on how to prepare yourself to confront a difficult subject, and then how to help others from a perspective of care and concern. This segment will provide biblical and theological insights for how we understand and talk about God in the midst of violence, standing with and for troubled or abused teens, listening as representatives of the community of faith, and how we break the collusion of silence about violence. This is the first section in the resource; read it first.

Follow that section with "Violence in the Bible" to continue your self-education of how the community of faith understands and makes meaning of the violence in the world inherited from the days of our earliest biblical stories.

The article "Legal Knowledge Is Key" points out crucial information that all adult workers with youth need to know to determine when, how, and what to do to protect themselves and their youth legally. When you suspect that a teen has been abused or victimized by violence, what are your legal responsibilities? What will happen if you must report and you do not? Be sure you become acquainted with the laws of your state.

TO THE POINT: *VIOLENCE*
Seizes Teachable Moments

Not every encounter with the subject of violence requires a full program on a related topic. But you still want to address that casual question, or the "pop in" visit by several teens to your office at church, or the encounter in the hallway.

The section, "Teaching Articles," provides lots of up-to-date information about manifestations of violence, like how our language contributes to a violent culture, inside scoop on gang activity, violence in the media, ritual abuse, and more.

You can read these articles for your own information and pass them along. Some of them may be reproduced and distributed without permission. If you want to do some intentional activities or begin a profitable discussion, the helps are right there, either on the same or the next page. Mine these articles for wisdom on how to be ready for the teachable moments that teens will offer you.

The articles and reflection sections are also suitable for a more formal setting, such as a youth group meeting, sharing group gathering, or other study setting.

We encourage you to pay special attention to the personal stories. Each provides a different slant, or set of values, or cluster of circumstances that will give teens multiple ways to reflect on their own values, behavior, and situations.

TO THE POINT: *VIOLENCE*
Offers Reference Material

In addition to worship resources, you have a section entitled "Where to Go for Help" that goes beyond simply listing agencies or printed resources. You also get help with how to go about connecting with agencies, how to recognize signs of abuse, and other statistical background data to make good decisions with and for your youth.

When Someone Comes to You

Being Pastoral

by Joretta Marshall

Standing with youth in the midst of a violent world implies that one walks on sacred ground with another. These moments of significance require adult friends who can take off their shoes and stand carefully, steadfastly, compassionately, and honestly. Youth are confronted daily with violence in individual and personal relationships and in the broader context of the world. Throughout their lives young people encounter the pain of shattered relationships, violent families, weapons fired in public places, and the reality of a world at war. Adult friends are essential companions as youth sort out their experiences and feelings.

Adult friends may also have legal responsibilities in the midst of caregiving. Be sure to read the article "Legal Knowledge Is Key" beginning on page 12.

Violence Is All Around Us

Violence appears in various forms: as someone suffers the continual verbal abuse of a parent, as a young person is traumatized by date rape, as a friend watches another die at the hands of an unknown assailant with a gun, or as the television records the onslaught of places where war is an everyday reality for youth and their families. The manner of violence in our society is without number.

Violence can manifest itself in the sophisticated forms of racism, sexism, or oppression, which are common elements of this culture. In these contexts persons carry internal scars resulting from a perpetual assault on their being. Silent survivors of sexual abuse, family violence, or aggression in dating relationships may leave wounds that few see from the outside as victims learn to hide or ignore their feelings. Fear, pain, or anger may fester inside someone's soul for years before it is acknowledged and processed in some meaningful way.

At other times violence is more evident as people bear witness to external scars in the form of broken arms, black eyes, and gunshot wounds. We are more likely to identify the manifestations of external violence. It is important to remember that external scars reflect the presence of internal pain and trauma.

The reality of violence in our world affects everyone in the community of faith, whether we are the personal victims of offensive actions who are identified easily or among the multitude who walk the streets with greater fear. Those who are bound together in the church cannot escape the call of the gospel to bring prophetic and pastoral voices to the actuality of the world in which we live.

Many questions and feelings arise when a young person approaches you to talk about personal experiences of violence or the manifestation of violence in the world. Pivotal to a balanced youth ministry is some reflection on how you might respond and what may be most helpful when someone comes to you. What do you say? Where do you turn for assistance? How do you decide when it is important not to keep a secret someone has confided to you? The difficult theological questions that arise in the context of dealing with violence are meaningful considerations as well. Where is God when violence happens? Why doesn't God stop the violence? Does God even care? Why does the church keep silent in the midst of a violent world?

These questions, along with others, are approached in this article from the perspective of one who is called to be a pastoral person in ministry with youth.

Being Pastoral

There are many reasons why someone might approach you to talk about a painful and difficult experience or share some of their feelings of fear or anger. Sometimes you are in the right place at the right time and the young person has decided that you can be trusted. Other times the person asking for assistance has reflected for a long time about the right person to talk with, seeking out someone trustworthy or in leadership in the church.

It is important to remember how difficult it is for most of us to share our deepest and most painful experiences and feelings. Courage and strength are required as people become vulnerable in talking about their stories. For some there is the added fear that talking about the violence might result in the perpetrator of that incident having to face accusation and restitution. This is particularly true if the offender is someone whom the youth knows personally. Most of us do not easily reveal the chaos of our lives when we fear that sharing the story might create pain in the lives of others. Far too many youth carry the stories of violence on the inside where few people are aware of their devastating power. Recognizing the amount of tenacity it takes for persons to open up and talk is an important first step in standing on sacred ground with youth.

As adult workers in the context of the church, we become pastoral representatives. The word *pastoral* is often misunderstood to indicate only those who are ordained ministers. Yet, *pastoral* is a word that reflects the care and shepherding by others within the context of the community of faith. Pastoral care should never be limited to the ordained clergy, but ought to be something in which others in the community of faith actively participate. Providing care from a pastoral perspective offers persons hope and sustenance based in the message of a gospel of care.

Adults within the church bear witness to the good news by participating in the life of the church, accepting positions of leadership within its ministry. The church cares about the pains of others not simply because it's the honorable thing to do, but because being present with others in the name of the gospel is the appropriate response to the call of God. When someone comes to you as a member of the church, you become, in turn, a representative of this broader community of faith. You do not act out of your own individual sense of faith, but out of the call of the community of which you are a part.

In similar ways, when someone comes to you in the context of the church, you become a representative of God, reminding persons of God's steadfast love and care. Individuals and communities of faith become the real and living symbols of a God who may seem far away and distant in the midst of tragedy, despair, and violence. One symbol of faith and hope is to reach out for someone who believes in God at a time when one may wonder about trusting God for one's self. As members of the church we symbolically sustain the faith and hope for persons in crisis when they may not be able to carry the load by themselves.

It is not unusual for someone in crisis to wonder whether God cares about individual pain, to be angry at God for not fixing the problem, or to be disappointed in God for not stopping the violence. These are natural responses to crazy-making situations in life and reflect the depth of one's pain. As the pastoral representative, it is not your duty to defend God or attempt to convince someone that God cares. Instead, pastoral caregivers embody the love of a God who hurts deeply when others are in pain. As you share the tears of a confusing journey, you are a representative of a God who does not magically take away pain or protect persons from harmful violence; rather you represent the God who cries tears, becomes angry at injustice, and faithfully stands with those who bear the internal or external scars of violence.

Persons struggling to make sense of the chaos of the world need faithful representatives who embody a pastoral care that is real and genuine, who are not afraid to

When someone comes to you in the context of the church, you become a representative of God, reminding persons of God's steadfast love and care.

ask difficult and incomprehensible questions, and who reflect the support of the broader community of faith. Traditionally the church has embodied its care through four significant activities: healing, sustaining, guiding, and reconciling. As pastoral representatives, adult workers with youth participate in these ongoing activities of the church, offering healing for those who are suffering, sustenance for those who are surviving and enduring, guidance for those in the midst of perplexing situations, and reconciliation between individuals and the broader world.

The Danger of Silence

Ministry requires that persons take the risk of breaking silences. The church has not always maintained open doors for persons who have experienced violence. Pain and trauma often make others uncomfortable, and there is a part of the church that would rather victims keep silent about their experiences. However, the church can no longer afford to keep silent about violence; the silence is killing our children, our world, and any possibility of living into a kin-dom of peace and justice. Indeed, the church's unwillingness to confront the violence may be killing God's spirit in the world.

Sometimes silence reflects our inability to do anything to take away the pain or hurt of another, or it may indicate the complexity of situations in which we become paralyzed. Other times the silence indicates our fear of "rocking the boat" or talking about issues that make others uncomfortable. Whatever the reason for our silence, the truth is that the church must represent a place where we are encouraged to face our fears, rather than turn our backs on the victims of violence. Without such honesty the church encourages people to keep silent about abuse and trauma, rather than inviting them into the healing presence of a community of faith and reconciliation that can uphold them in the journey. The church can never afford to be complacent in the midst of injustice and violence.

Silence can collude in sending a message to people about what they can and cannot talk about in the context of the church. When the church communicates that, it does not want to hear about other people's experiences of violence, we are guilty of passively perpetuating the world that supports violence. Marie Fortune, a prominent theologian puts it this way: "We allow abuse to continue by taking refuge in ideas that excuse us from action: assumptions that violence in human interactions is inevitable, that violence in families is not widespread but is to be expected, that no one *we* know is a victim or abuser, that decreasing the amount of violence in the world in general is unlikely and that eliminating violence in the family in particular is impossible." (From *Violence in the Family*, by Marie M. Fortune, The Pilgrim Press, Cleveland, 1991, pages 3-4. © 1991 by the Center for Prevention of Sexual and Domestic Violence. Used by permission.)

Finding ways to break the silence in youth groups is a major task in opening the doors for persons to come forward and share their experiences. One of the ways to break the silence is to offer discussion groups on painful topics before you encounter them in someone's story. For example, invite a worker in the domestic violence shelter or a counselor who treats survivors of sexual abuse to present a program. Keep resources in your library that are available and in plain view of youth. Lead your congregation through a curriculum dealing with some manifestation of violence. For example, utilizing Marie Fortune's *Violence in the Family: A Workshop Curriculum for Clergy and Other Helpers* provides a wonderful opportunity for reflection and opening of doors for persons to talk about their lives. Send a message to youth, their friends, and their families that you can talk about painful issues in the context of the church.

Moving from silence to openness in conversations encourages people to lament the reality of their lives and to shift from paralysis to active pastoral care.

There have been times in the history of the church when we have moved too quickly toward forgiveness without making persons accountable and responsible for the destruction that has been perpetrated.

Resources of the Community of Faith

Many perplexing questions and concerns arise in the context of dealing with violence, and it is imperative that pastoral caregivers lean on the resources of the community of faith. The following are not band-aids that can be applied randomly to fix things or take away the hurt and pain. They are blessings and gifts of grace that we carry in our souls as we engage persons in the midst of their faith journey.

▶ **The first resource is the community itself.** Adult workers with youth are not individuals doing a ministry in isolation; rather you are participants in a larger community that offers support and sustenance. Identify persons within the church who might be particularly helpful in dealing with the impact of violence. For example, who in your church is a mental health worker, a social worker, or a physician? To whom can you turn for legal advice? To whom can you refer youth and their families for ongoing counseling and support? Who sits on the board of the local domestic violence shelter or youth servicing agency?

Think about the persons in your congregation to whom you can turn for strength. Who prays for you and your ministry? To whom can you turn to share the tears and burdens of your heart?

▶ **The second resource of the community is found in the lives of other victims/survivors.** These are persons who have experienced violence and are in the process of healing. They can become role models and mentors to others. It is sometimes difficult to identify these persons because of the silence with which some survivors live. However, if you spread the word that you are in need of persons who can talk with youth about their own victimization, you may be surprised about who courageously responds to the call. This also offers survivors the opportunity to continue to enhance their lives as they share their strengths in surviving and thriving.

▶ **The third resource is our worship, both corporate and private.** Know the psalms of lament and use them regularly in worship with youth. Encourage people to think about persons who need to lament the violence in their individual or corporate lives. Make sure that public prayers of petition and healing are offered for the nameless numbers who have experienced forms of abuse and violence. Include in your prayers survivors of sexual abuse, domestic violence, street violence, or youth in countries where war is an everyday occurrence. Be careful and attentive about the content of your prayers. Do not offer magic, but speak prayers of the heart and soul that touch on the pain and despair of violence. Offer prayers that ask for healing of the body as well as the soul and mind.

Think carefully about prayers that might be offered for perpetrators of violence. One of the theological questions that arises in the midst of working with survivors of violence centers on issues of forgiveness. There have been times in the history of the church when we have moved too quickly toward forgiveness without making persons accountable and responsible for the destruction that has been perpetrated. Never pray for automatic forgiveness for persons who have been offenders of violence. Instead, find ways to pray for a person's honest confrontation of patterns of abuse or participation in the violence. Forgiveness is not a quick process, but is something that comes only with time and usually a great deal of work.

▶ **A fourth resource is that of theological reflection.** Engage persons in thinking about images of God that are healing and sustaining. Remind people of the God who is as the Mother Eagle who carries the young on her wings as they learn to fly, or the God who hears the cries and sheds tears for those who suffer and are in despair. It is imperative that those who work within the context of the church as leaders invite youth (and adults) into reflections about how one experiences and thinks about God.

Finally, within the context of the community of faith we have the opportunity to reflect about suffering and despair, hope and reconciliation, sin and forgiveness, and what it means to live in a world that works toward justice and peace. Offer hope that is based not in some kind of naive optimism, but a genuine hope born in the midst of painful living. Offer the vision of a world where violence is not the last word but where people work toward justice and protection of the vulnerable.

It is important in the church to reflect on these theological dimensions of life. How do we think about suffering and hope in the midst of a world where there is senseless violence every moment? How do we think about God's participation in suffering? Where is God when a child is senselessly killed or a teenager experiences sexual assault? How do we talk about forgiveness without making it cheap grace?

Community Resources

The broader communities of which we are a part have valuable resources to offer. You will want to become familiar with agencies that service youth or that deal with particular issues. Remember that part of the good news is that no one is called to fill all of the needs of every person and family within the youth group. We are called to be faithful witnesses who know the resources of the broader communities in which we live. This offers a wonderful model for youth about the importance of reaching out.

Again, identify counselors and workers within the town, county, or city who work specifically with youth issues. Know those who work in the area of domestic violence. Keep track of agencies in your communities that are working with those who live in the midst of street violence. Personally get to know these people by arranging to meet with them and learn about their services.

Persons in the community can also assist in educating you so that you know what to watch for in youth. There are external signs that someone is experiencing violence, is depressed, or is turning to drugs or alcohol to numb their pain. Participate in ongoing education so that you are aware of these indicators in the youth and families with whom you work.

It is helpful to know the persons who work in the educational systems. Being acquainted with the guidance counselors or others within the schools will assist in creating lines of communication and sources of referrals in the midst of crises. When a situation arises, you will not have to wonder who to contact but will already have established a supportive resource.

An Invitational Ministry

The ministry of working with youth is one of invitation. Providing the kind of space that invites people to be open is critical. Being a person whom youth trust and a person who exhibits an openness to have conversations about difficult and painful issues signals youth that you are approachable and will not be devastated or so surprised by what they tell you that they worry about your ability to handle their pain.

Think about what kind of space you have. Is it a place where people feel free to come and talk? Is it a place where people feel they can talk to you confidentially? Work to create an environment that is inviting and respectful of people's privacy.

Another important part of an invitational ministry is to be an adult who can be trusted. Think about your response to these questions: Do you keep confidences well? Are you able to be an adult friend, maintaining boundaries without trying to become one of the youth? Do the youth know that you are able to hear painful stories without becoming so emotionally caught up in the stories that you lose your grounding?

Honoring confidential information and keeping secrets are not necessarily the same things. There are times when persons want to know if you will keep a secret. Often youth and their families may share confidential information that ought to remain in your care. Honoring confidentiality is critical to youth ministry and implies that one does not talk about things that people tell you *unless* you are afraid for their safety or the safety of someone else. Keeping secrets, on the other hand, is dangerous when someone's physical, emotional, or sexual safety is at stake. If you have knowledge about abusive behavior or suicidal or homicidal intents, it is important that you immediately discern what to do with this information. In many states it is a legal requirement that persons report such information.

Never agree to keep a secret without knowing what is at stake. When someone wants you to promise not to tell before they will talk to you, offer them the opportunity to share their story and to think together about a plan of action. This way you invite them to participate in the activity of planning their own response to a situation. This empowers the youth as well as offers a way to be clear that you will not keep secrets if you are in fear of someone's safety.

If you suspect abuse or violence is occurring in someone's life, it is important to take initiative without becoming invasive. Find ways to open up conversations or ask directly if you are concerned about someone's physical, emotional, or spiritual safety. Know the laws in your state about reporting abuse. Do you have to report when you suspect abuse? Are you required by law to call the state department for youth services if you think there is a potential for violence in a family? Do you have a lawyer or someone in the congregation with whom you can consult about cases such as these? Reporting the abuse protects the victim and stops potential violence from occurring. It sends a message that violence will not be tolerated.

When Someone Comes to You

Marie Fortune offers the following advice about what to do when someone comes to you: 1) Listen and believe; 2) Assess the danger; 3) Make appropriate referrals and work cooperatively with other helpers; 4) Address pastoral concerns. (*Violence in the Family*, by Marie M. Fortune, The Pilgrim Press, Cleveland, 1991, pg. 82.)

▶ **Listen carefully.** It is imperative that workers with youth listen carefully and offer a place of sanctuary and safety as they tell their story. As you assess the current danger of a particular youth, find out if the abuse or violence is ongoing or something from the past. Are there other persons involved who might also be at risk? Who has the person already told about the abusive behavior? You will want to work immediately on an appropriate referral. Do not try to handle emotionally-charged issues by yourself. Again, remember that we are called as a community, not as individuals!

Youth need people who can hear their pain without withdrawing or becoming overly emotional. It is all right to share emotions and tears; however it is important to keep your wits about you so that youth know you will be steadfast and able to stand in the midst of the chaos and turmoil. When the world feels like it is falling apart, it is important to know that someone else is able to stand with you and be somewhat stable in the process.

▶ **Know yourself and monitor your feelings.** Know yourself well enough to know what your vulnerable areas are in working with others. For example, ask yourself about your ability to deal with emotionally-charged issues without overreacting. Have you worked through your own issues of sexuality and are you able to assist and support youth as they struggle with theirs? Does your family history make you more vulnerable to youth who need assis-

tance around domestic violence issues? Again, can you stand and remain steadfast when the world around you is crazy? This does not mean ignoring the feelings you have, but does suggest that you are able to recognize, name, and handle your feelings in ways that offer hope and sustenance to others rather than despair or paralysis.

▶ **Address and sensitize.** Keep confronting important issues and sensitive topics in your youth group. Recognize and talk about the difficulty of living in a violent world so that youth can process violence before it becomes personalized. Talk about the violence in the streets, in schools, in homes, and in the world.

▶ **Be honest about the strengths and weaknesses within any family.** Discuss honestly the struggles of being a family. Give people an opportunity to talk about their imperfect families. Do not pretend that every family who attends church is happy and without violence. This will invite those youth who may be struggling with some form of abuse or violence to come forward and talk about what is happening in their families.

▶ **Know when to open up a difficult discussion.** There are times when it is important to process things with a larger group of people, particularly if the effects of a particular experience of violence are broadly felt. For example, if a youth member is hurt or killed by an act of violence, it is critical that you offer persons the opportunity to gather together. It is not important at that point to figure out what you are going to do or how to organize a group activity. What is critical in helping others process trauma is that they have an opportunity to talk about their feelings from the experience. Know that some people will need to do more processing than others and be ready to hand out the names of other resources, persons, and counselors in the community. Remember, if your youth group has a history of talking about difficult subjects, they will be able to work more gracefully through other traumas.

Being involved in ministry with youth is a significant part of the ministry of the church. Healing is a process that takes a long time. Be prepared to walk the journey with people through painful moments and stand on sacred ground, offering the grace and care of God.

Joretta Marshall is on the faculty of Iliff School of Theology where she teaches pastoral care and counseling. A member in the Wisconsin Annual Conference, she is active in a variety of United Methodist functions. Joretta enjoys hiking and camping.

Norhill Photography © 1993. The photograph for this article features model(s) not the actual subject(s) of the story.

Legal Knowledge is Key

by Evelynn S. Caterson

"Ignorance of law is no excuse," so the saying goes . . . but for adults teaching and working with children and teenagers, ignorance of the child abuse laws is inexcusable! That failure to know may hurt both an abused teen and you.

The statutes dealing with child abuse prevention and child protection are primarily *state* statutes as opposed to *federal* or nationwide statutes. Usually federal law intervenes only in child abuse situations that cross state lines, such as in the distribution of child pornography. There is no one national child abuse law, but there are general questions and information that can help you as a teen counselor/leader gain adequate knowledge to protect both yourself and the teenager according to the law.

See the section "Where to Go for Help" on page 90 for more VERY important information about legal responsibility.

Civil Versus Criminal Child Abuse Law

Most states have two types of child abuse laws: one set for use by the child protection/social service agencies; the second set for criminal prosecution. In most states these two sets of laws in some way reference each other, although they are not usually printed together in the statute book. Most of the differences in statutes are found between the laws of the various states.

Even the definition of child abuse can vary. Consider these questions:

▶ Physical abuse by severe beating is child abuse nationwide, but what about forcing a teenager to do a great deal of physical labor?

▶ A parent's sexual intercourse with his or her teenager is child abuse, but what about exposing that same child to pornographic literature?

▶ Does your state define emotional abuse? Is putting too much pressure on a child to excel in sports or to get into college emotional abuse?

▶ In an economically depressed family is failure to feed and clothe a child abuse or a sad consequence of poverty?

What we think or feel can't substitute for the facts of the law. You must know state definitions and statutes.

Reporting

All fifty states have a law requiring at least certain persons, such as physicians, to report child abuse. Many states, however, require everyone and anyone to report suspected child abuse. All states deal with civil immunity for reporting child abuse, however the extent of civil immunity for each state varies and should be checked.

State statutes differ also about to whom the child abuse is to be reported. Further, if you are legally required to report child abuse, what triggers that requirement? The exact wording requirement is found in the state statute itself and the interpretation of the words of the statute is given by the courts that have dealt with the particular state statute. Both the statute and the case law should be checked. No state *requires* that the child abuse reporter have knowledge sufficient to convict the perpetrator nor that the reporter know who the perpetrator is.

What penalty is statutorily given for failure to report? Whether the reporting statute is listed in the criminal laws or the civil laws, the penalty is usually only criminal—a fine, probation, jail time. Civil liability for failure to report can only attach to someone who has a legal duty to report and a separate civil legal action would have to be filed. A duty-bound professional who fails to report child abuse may be looking at action by his or her ethics or licensing board. You should check your state laws to know under what circumstances you are duty-bound to report.

Proving Child Abuse and Court Action

Within any state the most significant differences between its child abuse criminal laws and its child protection laws are the amount and type of evidence needed to prove child abuse and what court action can be taken.

To prove criminal child abuse, like all other crimes, a specific defendant must be named and the proof of guilt must be found beyond a reasonable doubt. If a defendant denies the child abuse, the case could involve a public jury trial and personal, in court, testimony by the child victim. Once guilt has been found, the action of the Court is almost totally focused on the defendant, either in punishment or rehabilitation. The focus is not, and by law cannot be, on the victim or the victim's family, because the criminal court has jurisdiction only over the defendant before it—not the victim or family members.

In contrast, the child protection statutes allow a civil court (or family court or juvenile domestic relations court) to find that a child has been abused without needing to find exactly which family member did what. A child can be removed from his or her home immediately without the court having to first determine whether the abuser was a parent, a stepparent, a parent's boy or girlfriend, or even whether it was more than one person. The court action focuses on the best interest of the child, not on the punishment of the guilty, and the proof needed is only a preponderance of the evidence that the child has been abused.

Gathering the Evidence

Clearly, the gathering and documenting of evidence is best left to professionals. Once the suspected child abuse has been reported to the appropriate authority(ies) you should step aside. However, it is crucial that you know from the beginning moment what you are dealing with concerning the legal evidence of child abuse.

Physical signs, such as cigarette burns, strap or belt welts, or scars across the back, are obviously physical indicators of child abuse and can be reported without even speaking with the teen. The more difficult situation arises when the evidence comes about in conversation, and the importance of getting the actual facts or words of the teen is crucial. It may be that the teen is telling you something he or she has not told anyone else. Hearing this initial report makes you a fresh complaint witness and what the teen has told you may become evidence against the perpetrator in a trial. Write down everything the teen has said, and write it down *immediately,* sign it, and date it.

Also crucial is that the evidence be from the teen, not your words being placed in the teen's mouth. "Who?" "When?" "Where did it occur?" "What happened next?" "What did you do?" "What did you say?" "How did you react?" are good questions. Do not ask yes or no questions or those that make obvious the answer you want: such as: "She put her lit cigarette all over your arm, didn't she?" "He undressed you then, right?" While it is hard to resist asking such questions, the answers do a disservice to the teen and *any* subsequent legal dealing with the situation. It is also crucial that you not show horror, surprise, or shock when listening. These emotions can cause the teen either to exaggerate to hook you more, or to clam up and not tell everything.

Finally, in both the gathering of evidence and in simply being alert to the signs of child abuse, it is important to know the myths of child abuse—some perpetrated by the church, others enforced throughout society. (See page 92.)

Everything Has a Price

The complexity of the issues may make you want to back off and not get involved, although you may not have that option under the law, especially after a teen has confided in you. Anything that happens (or doesn't happen) has a price.

Potential Costs to the Adult Worker Who Helps

▶ Time (often lots and lots)

▶ Stress in dealing with one's own emotions and stress in not being able to "fix it"

▶ Lost friendships with teenager's family and their friends

▶ Hassles with the criminal justice system and the child protection agency

▶ Loss of naiveté about the extent of child abuse

Potential Costs to the Teen Who Is Not Helped

▶ Abuse will continue

▶ Likelihood of becoming an abuser

▶ Serious emotional problems

▶ Functional difficulties for life

▶ Other children in the family may be abused

Potential Costs to the Teen With Help

▶ Public exposure

▶ Family retaliation and rejection

▶ Feeling of total aloneness

With or without help, there is a cost to all children, regardless of age, who have been abused. While there is a cost to you and to the teen, the benefits of a leader's being aware, reporting, and getting involved are significant. With that involvement, it is likely that the abuse will stop; counseling can help overcome the teen's emotional scars; the teen can have a normal adult life; and other children in the family will not be abused.

Evelynn Caterson is a lifelong United Methodist and an attorney who is now in private practice. She has lectured on child abuse and its prevention all over the Northeast, and has conducted training in child abuse for United Methodist camp counselors and others who work with children and teens. Lynn is also one of the four lay members of the Judicial Council. Lynn is a wife, mother, youth choir director, and plant fanatic. She lives in New Jersey.

Violence in the Bible

Violence in the Bible

by Jann Cather Weaver

Violence—your girlfriend tells you her boyfriend forced her to have sex last night; your best friend is shot in a drive-by shooting while waiting outside a store for his mother; another student shot a teacher in the hall last week; the girl next to you in math class tried to kill herself; your mother is frequently beaten by your father—and on occasion he tries to beat you.

In the Beginning . . .

Violence is ever present in all our lives. We need not live in a war-torn country to know the pain and intimidation of violence. Even in turning to the Bible we find violence from the early chapters of Genesis— "Now the earth was corrupt in God's sight, and the earth was filled with violence (*chamas*)" **(Genesis 6:11)**.

The Bible narrates events of violence because events of violence permeate our lives. The presence of violence in Scripture does not, however, signify the approval of violence by God. Nor does it mean God is a violent or a violence-seeking God! Scripture recounts stories of violence not to sanction violence, rather to testify theologically on and against the violence of the world.

When taking the whole of Scripture—the Hebrew and Christian Scriptures together—God does not sanction violence. God never sanctions violence toward one another, other nations, nor does God rain down "divine violent punishment" upon people. In the Hebrew language, violence is *chamas*, a disruption of how God has ordered life! Violence disrupts relationship—relationship between peoples and God. *Chamas* reveals that violence is not a way of God, rather a way *against* God. (From *Expository Dictionary of Biblical Words,* by W.E. Vines © 1984 Thomas Nelson. Pages 451-52.)

And After the Beginning

Events of violence in Scripture cover all forms of violence. By the fourth chapter in Scripture, Cain has already killed his brother Abel **(Genesis 4:1-10)**. In early Israel, women, sisters, and daughters are raped or murdered by people they love **(Judges 11:29-40; 2 Samuel 13:1-14)**. The beloved King David contrives and orders the murder of the husband of a woman he desires **(2 Samuel 11)**.

In the Christian Scriptures, the nativity of Bethlehem is ravaged by the massacre of all male children under two years by King Herod the Great **(Matthew 2:13-16)**. John the Baptist is later beheaded by Herod's son, Herod Antipas, in a political execution **(Matthew 14:1-12)**. Jesus tells a parable of violence perpetrated by strangers upon an innocent victim **(Luke 10:29-37)** and prevents a mob execution of a woman caught in adultery **(John 8:1-12)**. A disciple commits suicide according to the Gospel of Matthew **(Matthew 27:1-10)**, and one traditional interpretation of the Crucifixion holds a vengeful God needing an ultimate sacrifice — his son! — to appease God's wrath.

Social violence, violence perpetrated and sanctioned by social institutions, is also addressed in Scripture. Numerous stories in Scripture tell of wars against other nations or social violence against groups of people, such as the Samaritans. In the Sermon on the Mount, Jesus tells of a more faithful stance to those whom the world considers enemies: "You have heard that it was said, 'You shall love your neighbor and hate your enemy.' But I say to you, Love your enemies and pray for those who persecute you" **(Matthew 5:43-44)**.

Violence Today as Then

The violence in Scripture is the violence of today. The Bible presents violence, however, not as a God-approved *means* to solving life's difficulties, but as an injurious and unjust actuality, as an obstacle to abundant life in a faithful, fulfilled community of people.

Many ideas about the true nature of God abound. Some people hold that God is a wrathful, violent deity who redeems through violence and works on the side of those who commit violence against others. Others believe that the Bible attests to a God who suffers with the victims of violence; a God who grieves, suffers, and takes action through all acts of violence.

If we believe, as Christians, that God revealed God's self in an ultimate way through the life, death, and resurrection of Jesus Christ, then how we understand the working of God in response to this violence will lead us to understanding the Bible's overwhelming stance toward violence.

The Crucifixion: Child Abuse or Grievous Tragedy?

One traditional interpretation of the crucifixion of Jesus Christ **(Matthew 26-27; Mark 14-15; Luke 22-23; John 13, 18-19)** depends on an interpretation of God as needing a sacrifice to appease God's anger against sinful humanity. This common understanding of the Crucifixion is known as *propitiation* or *sacrificial atonement,* meaning our sins (our separation caused by wrong doings) are forgiven by God because Jesus Christ took on the sacrifice required by God's anger.

Sacrificial atonement by the Crucifixion renders God a violent, angry God. In fact, God the "father" kills his own son in a fatal scene of child abuse! Is this the true nature of God?

Other understandings of the Crucifixion do not abide by such an understanding of God. Other understandings step outside of this divine child-abuse model of the Crucifixion and approach the Crucifixion as a gross tragedy outside of God's purpose for Jesus. God was so grieved by the Crucifixion of Jesus that God offered new life (the Resurrection) in *response* to humanity's rejection and execution of Jesus! God did not *require* Christ's death on the cross, rather God *countered* immense anguish in an amazing free gift of hope and new life to all people, expressly those who grieve and suffer, who are victims of violence and tragedy.

Jesus opened to us new ways of living with God in faithful communities, ways of compassion for strangers and victims of violence, ways of forgiveness for ourselves and others, ways of welcoming the outcast to the table of healing and hope. In all that Jesus Christ did — his teachings, healings, and way of living — he pointed back to the presence of a loving God in our lives. In this revelation we do not find a wrathful, violent God. We find a God who sides for the victim, who welcomes the stranger, who heals the outcast, and feeds the hungry. Surely this God did not need to kill God's own son in order for our sins to be forgiven.

Recognizing that there are valid understandings of the Crucifixion other than as propitiation provides us with a fresh angle at seeing the other events of violence in Scripture. One other traditional interpretation of the Crucifixion is as an atonement, or at-one-ment; the reconciliation of all persons with God. Because "in Christ God was reconciling the world to himself, not counting their trespasses against them" (**2 Corinthians 5:19**), what Jesus has endured has also been experienced and endured by God. If we believe as Christians that God revealed God's self in an ultimate way through the life, death, and resurrection of Jesus Christ, then it is crucial that we understand God as a compassionate, grieved God rather than an angry, violent God.

Consider the Scripture
■ Do you think God needed someone to die to forgive our sins? Why or why not?

■ What, do you imagine if that were your son on the cross, would be your response to this violence? What was God's response?

■ If Jesus lived a nonviolent life, why then was he so violently killed? What was Jesus' response to this violence?

■ What might Jesus' words, "My God, my God, why have you forsaken me?" (**Matthew 27:46**) mean? When have you felt like this? What was God's response to this question of Christ's? (Read **Psalm 22**.)

Cain and Abel: God Protects Even the Murderer

In **Genesis 4** we read the account of Cain murdering his brother Abel. God hears the spilled blood of Abel cry out and demands that Cain confess what he has done. In response God banishes Cain to become "a fugitive and a wanderer on the earth" (**Genesis 4:12**) in the land of Nod (Wandering), east of Eden.

Yet Cain pleads his case before God, claiming "anyone who meets me may kill me" (**4:14**). Cain, who has killed Abel, fears being killed, but God does not kill him. In reading further we discover that God actually puts a mark on Cain "so that no one who came upon him would kill him" (**4:15**).

The God who grieved Abel's murder, who loved Abel and could hear Abel's blood cry out from the ground, who exiled Cain—a God of the victim—is also the God who stopped further violence and murder by marking (protecting) Cain. The God of the victim is the God of the exiled victimizer. God stops violence rather than seeking revenge through more violence.

This is not a God who enacts an eye for an eye. The God revealed to us in **Genesis 4** is a God who uses power to *restore* life rather than further *destroy* life by upholding violence.

Consider the Scripture
■ Why, do you think, did Cain kill Abel? Is this reason sensible? Why or why not?

■ Did Cain have any other choices than murdering Abel? What might they be? Apply those choices to a current situation of violence. Do Cain's reasons justify that current situation? Why or why not?

■ What would our society do to Cain, and how is that different from what God did to Cain? How can we act more like God than like Cain?

The Rape of Tamar: Secret Violence

The daughter of King David, Tamar, is forcibly raped by her half-brother, Amnon (**2 Samuel 13:1-22**). Claiming to have fallen in love with her (**13:1**), Amnon uses his powers to isolate Tamar from all who could protect her, and forcibly rapes her: "But he would not listen to her; and being stronger than she, he forced her and lay with her" (13:14).

Immediately following, however, Amnon is "seized with a very great loathing" (13:15a) for Tamar, a loathing more powerful than "the lust he had felt for her" (13:15b). He demands she be taken away as she begs him not to commit this even greater wrong of shaming her. Again Amnon would not listen. Tamar is cast out, leaving her to grieve (ashes on her head and tearing of her robe are signs of grief) by herself (13:19).

Tamar's full brother, Absalom, hearing her grief, tells Tamar to be quiet and not take the rape to heart because it was *only* her brother Amnon who raped her. King David, Tamar's father, was angry with Amnon but did not take action against Amnon for his violence against Tamar.

Violence happened in the family and everyone— even the most powerful person in the land, the king—held it a secret.

Consider the Scripture

■ What does this text tell us about the difference between making love and rape? What is the difference between love (13:1) and lust (13:15)?

■ What forms of violence happened in this rape? (*sexual violation, secrets and silence, not listening to Tamar, Absalom's words to Tamar, King David's lack of response*) What might be God's response to these forms of violence?

■ How is this story like date rape? incest? any other form of sexual violence?

Suicide: Violence to Self

Although suicide, especially teen suicide, is a reality of overwhelming proportion, the Bible recounts only a few instances of suicide. A careful reading of these Scripture narratives of suicide (1 Samuel 31:1-7; 2 Samuel 17:21-23; 1 Kings 16:15-20; Matthew 27:3-10) clearly reveals the absence of any direction by God to commit suicide. God's voice is absent from all the texts; the narratives merely recite the event.

The first suicide in Scripture is the suicide of King Saul in battle (1 Samuel 31:1-7). In a close reading of the text, however, the voice of God, that is, the desire or design of God, is absent from the narrative. This absence is indicative of God's lack of direction in Saul's action; Saul's suicide was not desired or required by God.

Yet we cannot assume that the lack of God's voice in the narrative indicates the lack of God's ultimate presence. First Samuel 31:11-13 indicates the faithful and honorable treatment of one in death, not the fate of one who died in disgrace. Saul's suicide, while clearly not the design or desire of God, did not vanquish Saul from God's love or from his own community of faith.

In Acts 16:25-34 the Apostle Paul prevents the suicide of his jailer and converts him to Christ. The text in quick action moves the jailer from utter despair to a newly baptized believer in God. The witness of love for the jailer by Paul and Silas brings the jailer to his knees, seeking that relationship with God that saves us all from hopelessness and death.

The Psalms reveal a God who knows us and follows us as a shepherd and counselor (Psalm 23). Psalm 139 assures us of a God who seeks us regardless of where we might flee. The teachings of Jesus, in particular, point to a God who seeks the lost (Luke 15, for example), desires abundant life for all (John 10:10), and who weeps at the sight of death (John 11).

Above all else, God wills life. This is the Resurrection, the good news of the gospel: from life's most horrible realities God can and will create hope and new life. The Scriptures neither specifically prohibit nor censure suicide. Rather, the Bible emphasizes the value of life and the care of God for all God's people in this life and in the next. In all of life and death, in all grief, trial, and tragedy, God is compelled by God's love to give us new life in ways beyond our imagining.

Consider the Scripture

■ As you look at the different stories, what circumstances surround the decision of the person to take his own life? What information is given and what details are missing?

■ Did any of these persons seem to be thinking about God or their families?

■ Is there any value-related comment in the Scripture that indicates approval or disapproval? If so, what are they?

■ What, do you think, are the reasons people commit suicide? What, do you think, would God say to these reasons? Why?

■ Do you think suicide is a valid way to resolve difficulties? Do you think God can help us resolve our difficulties in some other way? Give reasons for your answers.

For Further Reflection

Choose one or more of the selected Scripture texts below and compare it to a contemporary example. Use this exercise also with literature, music, television programs, and films that reflect (critically or not critically) violence in our world. Be sure you have commentaries on hand to help understand these passages and their contexts, especially since the cultural understandings are quite different from ancient to modern days.

After selecting the text, answer these questions:

■ Who is involved? Who has power? Who makes decisions?

■ What is the cultural context and how is it alike or different from today?

■ Who misuses power? How? Who are the victims? How do the victims respond?

■ How does God or Jesus Christ respond to the victim? to the one who causes violence?

■ What does the text tell you about dealing with violence today?

Domestic Abuse, Incest, and Child Abuse: **Genesis 16:1-16; 21:9-21** or **Judges 19:1-30**
Sexual Violence: **2 Samuel 13:1-22** or **John 8:1-11**
Murder: **Genesis 4:1-16** or **2 Samuel 11:1-27**
Political Violence: **Matthew 2:7-18** or one of these three: **Matthew 14:1-12; Mark 6:14-29; Luke 9:7-9**
Violence by Strangers: **Luke 10:29-37**
Suicide (Self-Violence): **Matthew 27:1-10**
Religious Violence: One of these four: **Matthew 26-27; Mark 14-15; Luke 22-23; John 13, 18-19** or **Acts 6:8; 7:51—8:3**

To Expand Your Thinking

Adultery throughout the time of the Bible was "the violation of a husband's right to have sole sexual possession of his wife and to have the assurance that his children were his own." (From *The Interpreter's Dictionary of the Bible* © 1962 Abingdon Press, Vol. 1, page 51.) Adultery was a violation of one of the Ten Commandments (**Deuteronomy 5:18; Exodus 20:14**).

If both parties were willingly involved in adultery, they could be sentenced to death (**Deuteronomy 22:22**). However, the death sentence could be invoked only with the evidence of two or more witnesses (**Deuteronomy 17:6**). Jesus alone could not, by law, condemn the woman, since neither he nor anyone else claimed to be a witness.

War and conquest are a prevalent part of the Old Testament story, especially in the conquest of the land of Canaan as written in Joshua and Judges, and later with the early nations of Israel and Judah as written in the books of Samuel, Kings, and Chronicles. Israel saw the conquest of Canaan as a divine intention, and native Palestinians are still trying to regain some of their own land.

The successful wars against Israel and Judah were understood as the punishment of God for their sinfulness. Regardless of the instigator or the victor, the wars described were begun with both sides invoking the power of their own deity or deities, including God. The results were usually brutal and bloody.

Sacrifice was an ancient religious practice stemming back to the earliest days of the Hebrew nation. While very complex psychologically and sociologically, sacrifices accomplished several things: offering gifts of honor or tribute to God; providing nourishment; symbolically re-establishing a right relationship with God after someone sinned or violated a law.

In early Palestinian religion, human sacrifice was commonplace and Hebrew Scriptures repeatedly denounced human sacrifice as antithetical to God's desires (for example, **Leviticus 20:2; 2 Kings 16:2-3; and Ezekiel 16:20-21**).

Suicide is rare in the Scriptures, and the biblical witness implies more that it specifically says about death by suicide. As with all passages, the ones relating to suicide deserve study in context—who narrates the event, what is said, what is not said.

The biblical commentary on suicide is consistently neutral. In ancient Greek and Roman thought, suicide could be considered a noble option, even a means of immediate salvation. Nearly one thousand Jewish loyalists committed suicide at Masada in the early first century rather than be taken prisoner or killed by the Roman army, and they are remembered as heroes.

The notion of suicide as a sin and a crime took shape well after the completion of the Bible, beginning around the fourth century with Augustine. What may be of greatest importance for teens is that suicide is not the answer to life's difficulties. The answer lies with God and with the community of the faithful as they support and affirm others in ways that promote abundant life.

Jann Cather Weaver is Associate Dean for Student Life at Yale Divinity School. Jann is a UCC ordained clergywoman having served parishes in the Wisconsin Conference. Jann received her Master of Divinity at Eden Theology Seminary in St. Louis and her Ph.d. in Theology and the Arts from the Graduate Theological Union in Berkeley, CA. Jann also teaches Film as Theology. In her spare time she is a scuba diver and studies Spanish.

Teaching Articles

Language and Violence

by Laurel Schneider

"Sticks and stones may break my bones, but words will never hurt me." Have you heard this old saying before? You may have been taught to say it as a child whenever someone called you names, put you down, or humiliated you. Saying it let them know that their taunts and insults didn't stick. But is the saying true? Sometimes, words *are* violent. Wars have been started and lives have been destroyed by words. When are words "just words" and when are words violent?

The Wheel of Violence

Learning about physical violence in our homes, cities, and world means that we must look closely at the attitudes and habits that make violence possible and acceptable. The use of violence is like the rim on a wheel, and power is the axle. People use violence to gain power and to keep control. Violence holds the wheel together by keeping people afraid, but physical violence is only one part of the picture; it is only the rim of the wheel. There are many spokes on the wheel that give violence power, which makes the wheel strong. One of those spokes is language—the words we use that make violence acceptable to us.

An Advocate for Peaceful Words

One of the greatest Christian leaders of our time, Dr. Martin Luther King, Jr., understood that violence can only work when people believe the words behind it. Violence supports racism in this country. Americans of African descent were regularly called demeaning names, and these names helped to make the violence of racism seem at least tolerable to most people. Dr. King helped Americans to begin taking the spokes out of the wheel of racism when, like Malcolm X, he started insisting on different words for African Americans, like *equal*, *human*, *decent*, and *beautiful*." Violence became harder to justify in the presence of these words. King refused to use insulting language, he refused to intimidate or threaten. Like Jesus, he refused to use violence against violence, and he saw that words even more than whips and fire hoses were keeping the violence of racism alive in America.

A Radical Against the Hurtful Word

Jesus made clear to his followers that the words they said were more powerful than sticks or stones. He told them that "it is not what goes into the mouth that defiles a person, but it is what comes out of the mouth that defiles" (**Matthew 15:11**). When he said this, Jesus was not only concerned about the purity of his many disciples, but about their understanding of violence. What you say *matters*. "Do you not see," he argued, "that whatever goes into the mouth enters the stomach, and goes out into the sewer? But what comes out of the mouth proceeds from the heart . . . For out of the heart come evil intentions, murder, adultery, fornication, theft, false witness, slander" (**Matthew 15:17-19**).

When you condemn a person with your words, even in fun or to impress your friends, you are condemning yourself, according to Jesus' way of looking at things. When a group of men were about to stone a woman to death because they had decided she was an adulteress (a word that meant death at that time) Jesus wanted them to see the violence of the word and demanded that only the one without sin could stone her. Of course all could think of wrongs they had done at one time or another, and not wanting the very treatment they were so ready to give out, one by one they left, leaving only Jesus. As the only one without sin, it was apparently within his rights to condemn and stone her (as long as there was a witness) but he chose instead not to call her any name, urging her simply to take care and not sin (**John 8:2-11**). He did not ask her if the charges were true. *He chose not to label her*. Why? The violence of a word was about to kill her and make killers of a group of men, and apparently Jesus didn't think that would help anybody.

Making outcasts of people with words, or killing them because of words, seemed to bother Jesus a lot. He went to great lengths to eat with the people he wasn't supposed to eat with, talk with the people he wasn't supposed to talk with, and generally hang out with the people nobody wanted to be seen with. Just as with the woman called an adulteress, Jesus didn't seem interested in telling these people what sinners they were. He seemed more interested in *un*-labelling them. It may be hard to imagine living your life without labelling people. Even Christians seem to love to label people—who is "in" and who is "out," who is good and who is bad. But when we do, we can't turn to Jesus for support. He deeply respected language and saw how violent even the smallest words, names, labels, or oaths can be. We all suffer, Jesus might say, when "the littlest of these" is called any of the violent names we hear every day.

The Power of *My* Words

Everyday language can be violent when it diminishes others. We commonly minimize the effects of language by saying things like "I was just joking" or "everybody says that." The problem is that we stop paying attention to the power of our words. It is common sense that children who are told that they are stupid or inferior grow up believing it about themselves and behave as if it were true. They tend to study less hard, to set low goals for themselves, and therefore achieve less and less. Teenagers and adults are just the same. When you begin to believe a label that is given to you or others, it becomes easier to look the other way when hurtful or violent actions occur. Names and labels separate people.

Words, true or untrue, have enormous power and can make even terrible violence seem acceptable. Emotional and physical violence are closely related. You may not have thought before that language has much to do with violence. Language is a support system for violent actions. It is very difficult to be violent toward someone you respect. Even violence at home, between people who say that they love each other, involves emotional abuse, name-calling, and labelling. Disrespectful and hurtful words allow for disrespectful and hurtful actions. They make violence seem okay, or even necessary.

Abusive language shifts the blame so that the violent person or persons can say that they had no choice. We talk ourselves into violence, and we talk ourselves out of responsibility for it. Jesus called each of his disciples to "love one another" as he had loved them. And how did he love them? Without labels. He knew how powerful words can be. Sticks and stones may certainly break bones, but words can make it possible.

For Further Reflection

Use the following questions and activities to reflect on the key points in the article.

How has language affected you?

■ What hurtful things have been said to you in the past? How did those words affect you? What did you do? How did you feel about yourself? about the one who spoke ill of you? What violent things have you said? How did it make someone else feel? What did you learn?

What effect does the language of others have?

■ Have you ever heard someone you respect, like a coach or a teacher, put someone down or say hurtful things about others, even in jest? How did it make you feel? How do you think those who heard felt? What kind of actions do you think became more acceptable in relation to that person or group afterwards?

■ Do you ever hear jokes that make violence toward someone seem normal? What are the worst labels in your school or group of friends?

■ What words or phrases do you hear at school, at home, or on TV that make violence seem normal? Try listing them. How often do you hear the words *kill*, or *beat up*?

■ Have you ever heard someone justifying their violent actions by calling people names? What was their reasoning? How did you feel about it? What did you think?

■ Try to think of some words that make violence more acceptable. For example, just think what kinds of violence our society has accepted and even supported when the word enemy has been used. What about using racial, ethnic, sexual, and economic slurs? How can these words lead to violence?

Do some awareness exercises

☞ For several days listen to the ways you and others use violent images in ways that seem playful or even affectionate, such as threatening to spank someone or teasingly offering to kill someone. What does our casual use of these images in friendly or loving situations mean?

☞ Write down all of the violent words you have used in anger or other negative ways, and a note about the context. Talk about it in a group. Has your violent language helped or hurt you? someone else? Has it encouraged a fight or extended beyond its original situation? What happened and why?

Think about what Jesus would think, say, or do

☞ Review the article for insight to Jesus' approach to violence. What other Scriptures speak about nonviolence? What would Jesus think about the violent nature of American culture? What difference does your faith make in your choice of words?

Laurel Schneider is currently pursuing her doctorate in theology at Vanderbilt University in Nashville, Tennessee. A native of Massachusetts, she received her M. Div. at Harvard and served a United Church of Christ parish in Cambridge, MA. She has contributed to several publications on issues of theology and society.

Media and Violence

by Todd Outcalt and Diana L. Hynson

Teenagers are bombarded by violence every day through the mass media. American teenagers not only watch about four hours of tension-filled television each day but also play with action-packed video games, listen to music that often contains violent themes, and even witness other types of violence in their homes and schools. (From *Media&Values*, No. 62, p. 8. The Center for Media & Values, 1962 Shenandoah St., Los Angeles, CA 90034) Many of the movies teens watch are centered around action heroes who machine gun their way through crowds of people.

The Working Group on Media at the National Consultation on "Safeguarding our Youth: Violence Prevention for Our Nation's Children," 1993 meeting reports our social effects that need to be considered in a discussion on media violence:

▶ **Increased aggression and meanness**—there is a "correlation between seeing mediated violence and being more violent now or in the future."

▶ **Victim effect**—"there is an increase in fear and concern for self-protection."

▶ **Bystander effect**—"there is an increased callousness and insensitivity to those around us who may be hurting."

▶ **Increased appetite for violence**—the more violence one sees, the more "jolts per minute" needed to keep viewers involved—and watching. Media violence can be addictive. (From The Center for Media and Values.)

The Grim Statistics

Certainly our children are exposed to high doses of violence through the various media forms—a much higher number of violent acts, in fact, than actually exists in real life. Consider these grim statistics from *Media&Values*, Number 62:

▶ The National Institute of Mental Health, after over ten years of study, states "The consensus among most of the research community is that violence on television does lead to aggressive behavior by children and teenagers who watch the programs" (page 9).

▶ By age 18, the average child has seen more than 200,000 violent acts, including 15,000 murders. Guns are the usual weapon of choice (pages 5 and 8).

▶ Cartoons and toy commercials average about 25 violent acts per hour, the highest rate on TV (page 8).

▶ MTV, USA, and HBO have six to eight times more acts of violence per hour than PBS and the networks (adjusting for the program *Top Cops*) (page 10).

▶ The most violence-filled TV hours:
6:00 - 9:00 am.- 165.7 acts per hour
2:00 - 5:00 pm.- 203 acts per hour
8:00 -11:00 pm.- 106 acts per hour (page 10).

The impact that this media violence is having, especially on our children, is the topic of much discussion today. Many parents, school officials, social agencies, and church members are wondering if television violence is playing a role in the steady rise of violent youth-related crimes. Do young people become desensitized to violence and death by watching movies like *Robocop*, *Terminator 2*, and *Last Action Hero*? Is the violence portrayed in certain MTV videos emulated by some teens? Are song lyrics about murder and mayhem and rioting contributing to the upsurge in these violent acts? The unfortunate answer is an unquestionable *yes*.

Media Literacy

Sister Elizabeth Thoman, Executive Director of the Center for Media and Values based in Los Angeles, California, in addition to doing much research pertaining to the relationship between the media and violent behavior, is also pioneering new ways of thinking about the influence and impact of the media in American society. This organization's goal is to provide media literacy education that can help people understand the impact of images in our life and culture.

Ms. Thoman identifies four key concepts that underlie media literacy education.

▶ *Media construct reality*. "All media are constructions and somebody has put it together, whatever it is—the nightly news, a TV sitcom, a daily newspaper, a billboard. In the process, some pictures are selected and others are rejected; some words remain, others are edited out; some scenes stay in, others end up on the cutting room floor. But, whatever is left, what the viewers sees, becomes a version of reality."

▶ *Media use identifiable techniques.* "One way to see how media makers construct reality is to take apart the world they create by identifying camera angles, music, special effects, costumes—things that heighten our response and grab our attention." By tuning in to these devices, we see how and why something claims our interest. In the process, we become smarter than the medium and less susceptible to its enticements.

▶ *Media are businesses.* Corporations spend billions of dollars on advertising, but what is really sold is the viewer. The heart of commercialism is the selling of time to advertisers—what we might call the "renting of eyeballs." The end all of programming is not entertainment, but the assurance that a certain number of consumers will see the advertising.

▶ *Media contain ideologies and value messages.* There is no such thing as value-free media; all contain points of view, and certainly not all of them are negative. There is, however, "lots of bias and hidden messages" about gender, race, ethnicity, and age within "harmless" entertainment. "To be media literate is to learn to separate the legitimate pleasure of being entertained from the subtle ideological messages about life that are embedded in those entertainments."
(Selected excerpts from "Violence: the Media Connection" by Elizabeth Thoman. From *Christian Social Action*, June 1993. © 1993. Used by permission.)

Educating ourselves and our young people about media violence is one way of taking control of the impact such images have upon our society. Helping teenagers to think about advertising and violence as they see it on television, and as they experience it in real life, is a first step toward gaining a healthier media relationship.

After all, not all images of violence are necessarily bad in and of themselves. Take, for example, a documentary about the Civil War. In such a movie we would see detached arms and limbs, the aftermaths of historical battles. We might also watch a movie about the Holocaust and witness similar atrocities of the human race. But these images, while disturbing, are necessarily a part of our education and knowledge of the world in which we live. The violent images found in movies like *Rambo* and *Terminator* are meant to entertain and shock, not to educate. Talking about the differences is a first step toward media literacy.

More Than Entertainment

Mental health experts have confirmed that television and movie violence encourages teenagers to act aggressively. The reasons for this are many. Not only do television and the movies promote violence as an acceptable form of behavior, but aggressive acts are often idealized as a primary means of problem solving. Violence is also portrayed in glamorous and unrealistic ways. And the "true to life" crime stories that are prevalent in today's movies do little to educate us about the deeper issues inherent in the problems that give rise to violent behavior in our society. Instead we get "jolts per minute."

> *Educating ourselves and our young people about media violence is one way of taking control of the impact such images have upon our society.*

"Jolts per minute" programming is often cited as a principle—almost a first law—of commercial television. "Jolt" refers to the moment of excitement generated by a laugh, a violent act, a car chase, quick film cut—any fast-paced episode that lures the viewer into the program. Television and screen writers often inject a jolt into their scripts to liven up the action or pick up the pace of a story.

Measuring the jolts per minute is a good way to discover how violence is used to keep the viewer's interest. When we consider the sheer number of violent acts we're exposed to for the sake of maintaining our attention, we can begin to understand how we're "jolted" into believing that the only thing that can keep our interest *is* violence. Here are some things you can do to keep from getting over-jolted:

☞ Ask yourself what type of jolts of violence are most common. Are there some that are more persuasive than others? Consider alternatives to using violent jolts. Would a joke work in place of a fist fight? How will this affect the story?

☞ Observe the promos for upcoming television shows. Are the clips mostly scenes of violence? Do the promos get more violent at certain hours?

☞ MTV has gained a reputation for quick edits and splashy graphics. How many of these cuts are scenes of violence? Are the quick cuts themselves acts of violence to our senses? What types of videos use more jolts of violence than others? (From *Media&Values*, No. 62, page 7. The Center for Media and Values, 1962 Shenandoah St., Los Angeles, CA 90034.) *Based on media awareness activities in* Media Literacy Resource Guide 1989, *Ministry of Education, Ontario, Canada.*

Media Literacy as Violence Prevention

Media perceptions do not help us to deal with the problem of violence in preventive ways. Rather, we are often given images of violence through movies and television that combine humor with killing and destruction. In the movie, *Total Recall*, after the husband (played by Arnold Schwarzenegger) shoots his wife, he cracks a joke on the way out: "I guess you can consider this a divorce!" These images deny the reality of death in life, deny that there are funerals, tears, pain, bloodshed, terror, or children who have lost a parent.

The Center for Media and Values is producing a multimedia educational resource package *Beyond Blame: Violence in the Media*. Elizabeth Thoman points out five ways that media literacy can contribute to lessening the impact and incidence of violence in our lives.

▶ **Reduce exposure to media violence** particularly of the young, by educating parents and caregivers about the issue and helping them to develop and enforce age-appropriate viewing limits.

▶ **Change the impact of violent images that are seen**—by deconstructing the techniques used to stage violent scenes and decoding the various depictions of violence in different genres—news, cartoons, drama, sports, and music.

▶ **Locate and explore alternatives** to storytelling that highlight violence as the preferred solution to human conflict.

▶ **Uncover and challenge the cultural, economic, and political supports for media violence**—militarism, greed, competition, dominance, structural poverty—as well as the personal ways we may each be contributing to the creation or perpetuation of a mediated culture of violence. Media literacy empowers its partici-

Media literacy empowers its participants to ask hard questions of themselves, of others, and of society, by applying the principles of critical thinking to experiences that look like "mindless entertainment."

pants to ask hard questions of themselves, of others, and of society, by applying the principles of critical thinking to experiences that look like "mindless entertainment."

▶ **Break the cycle of blame and promote informed and rational public debate about these issues** in schools, community and civic gatherings, religious groups, and the media itself. An informed public is less vulnerable to extremist views or actions.

For Further Reflection

A good way to begin discussing the issue of media violence with teens is to use actual television shows, movies, and videos that demonstrate some aspect of the problem.

Lead a general discussion about media and violence.

■ How does the evening news reflect our eagerness to hear about murder and violence? What images usually headline the news on television?

■ Can you recall any real life acts of violence that were influenced by media images or themes in the last ten years (such as a murder mimicking one on TV)?

■ Why do you think the media prefers to present a "good-guy, bad-guy" scenario to violence rather than the reality that most violence is committed between persons who know each other? How do our attitudes fuel and allow the media to do this so easily?

Media Mania
☞ Divide your group into pairs. Give each pair several cards containing the names of recent movies or television shows (particularly violent ones). Ask each pair to choose one they both have seen and discuss why this medium was so popular. After pair discussion, allow each pair to share with the larger group their observations. Ask these questions:

■ Do you think these shows have any impact upon behavior in our society? Why or why not?

■ How do you feel immediately after watching a violent or scary show? later at home? the next day?

■ Look at the box on "jolts per minute." What do you recall about the jolts in the show?

■ Identify the techniques used to construct the reality. How "real" is that reality?

Investigate ways the violence could affect behavior.
■ How many times was violence rewarded? How?

■ How realistically was the violence displayed? Who was victimized the most? the least? Why?

■ How much violence was used by the "good guys"? by the "bad guys? How did you feel when someone used violence to solve a situation?

■ How often was violence justified or glorified? In what situations do you think the means justified the ends? Why?

■ Did the violent characters do something you do or want to do? What does that tell you?

List your own viewing guidelines.
☞ Using posterboard, ask group members to make a list of some guidelines that would be helpful in determining which programs, movies, or other media to watch and/or how to process our thoughts and feelings after we have watched something disturbing.

Examine biblical images.
☞ Ask students to read some of the more violent episodes found in the Bible
Exodus 2:11-16 (Moses murders an Egyptian)
Judges 11:29-31, 34-39 (Jephthah sacrifices his daughter)
2 Samuel 11:2-4, 14-17 (King David's sins)

■ What do these stories tell us about the nature of evil and violence? What can give rise to violent behavior?

■ Do you think these stories would make good movies?

■ Are there underlying positive messages to be gained from these violent stories of the Bible?

■ How would you describe the people involved in these violent acts: Moses, Jephthah, David?

☞ Try writing a movie script that will preserve the integrity of the Biblical story, but also teach a lesson.

Much of the information in this article has been quoted or adapted from information supplied from the Center for Media and Values, most especially from the magazine *Media&Values: A Cornerstone of the Media Literacy Movement,* Number 62. This magazine is part of the resource kit. For additional information about *Beyond Blame* or other resources produced by the Center for Media and Values, contact the Center for Media and Values, 1962 S. Shenandoah St., Los Angeles, CA 90034 or call (310) 559-2944.

Todd Outcalt is a United Methodist pastor in the South Indiana Conference. For the past five years he has taken youth on mission trips to Denver, Dallas, Canada, Milwaukee, and Louisiana. Todd lives in Indiana with his wife, Becky; daughter, Chelsey; and son, Logan.

Diana L. Hynson is an editor with the Department of Youth Publications at The United Methodist Publishing House in Nashville, TN. Diana has edited and contributed to several youth publications.

Living With Fear

by Diana L. Hynson

I asked three young people who are about to enter middle school what they expected at the new school. What followed was war story after war story of experiences that reveal a climate of violence in their schools. At age twelve, Jenna, Josie, and Amy are becoming sophisticated observers and analysts of their own culture as a means of self protection and preservation, while doing what most of us think should be a relatively hazard-free occupation—attending school.

"Good People and Bad People"

"Good" people can become "bad" people. Hanging out with a different crowd can change one's status in a hurry. But it's the bad people who bother, harass, threaten, rob, and hurt good people or other bad people who committed some indiscretion.

The distinctions between the good ones and the bad ones can be quite clear. The bad people are the trouble-makers, the bullies, the ones who push until a fight starts and then declare themselves the winner regardless of who won. Winning gets defined in ways that particularly suit the so-called victor, and winning is a paramount goal. The bad people have reputations to uphold and a certain pugnacious status to maintain. They are the ones who might have been good once, but got tired of being the object of someone else's bad attitude and crossed over. "If you can't beat 'em, join 'em" has a whole new meaning here.

Amy, Josie, and Jenna talked about their elementary school experience. They expect this pattern to remain the same in middle school. Being in a school with changing classes adds to the vulnerability because students are in common areas, like the halls, more often. They have heard stories from their brother; he's been there.

Is it always so easy to tell who's a bad person and who's a good person? These kids hear who was caught with a weapon. They recognize some of the druggies—the ones who sell, the ones who want to buy, and the ones who hassle the good people who have never used drugs. They are aware of who has been suspended or who picks a fight for the fun of it. The network of communication in the school is fast, if not always accurate. Never knowing when one of the bad people is going to hassle or hurt you contributes to a climate of fear.

The Games We Play

Using the network for misinformation is one of the games that can get violent. At the beginning of the school day, two gangs or cliques set up a "war." It might start with a deliberate lie or rumor about someone. The game is played throughout the day by "recruiting"; that is, seeing how many people will be on each side by the end of the day. Usually the "war" is between same sex factions. The pattern contributes to a willingness, if not a need, to buddy up, take sides, and compete in order to survive. Being on the side with the least supporters may mean getting beat up at the end.

Dares also add to the violent atmosphere. Someone's violence is just "fun." Sometimes it's the result of a dare. One bully dares another and someone else gets caught in the middle. Seems like the bully never gets picked on. Another reason to turn from good to bad.

Misdirection or starting rumors is a potentially volatile past time too. This game is played by deliberately telling a lie about someone to retaliate for some grievance, real or imagined. If a vocal lie is not the preferred option, writing the person's name on school property can be just as effective. When the administration discovers the name, they assume it is an autograph, and the bearer of that name is in for it. And no one can really control having their name appear in a public place, although they can fear it and the consequences.

"If You Touch Someone, They'll Beat You Up"

Any misstep can be hazardous to your health. Something as minor as accidentally brushing up against someone in the hall can result in being beat up. Being in one of the arts programs, like music, may not be cool enough—another potential misdemeanor; another way to incur negative attention.

A big mistake is tattling. Or talking about someone else. Or making fun. Or staring. All these activities focus attention on someone who may not like it or who is only too glad to mention it to someone else who won't like it. Words have a way of coming back to haunt, so it doesn't pay to make an offhand or malicious remark. The price can be a beating.

Guilt by association (or disassociation) can be

unhealthy too. Having an older sibling at the same school may not be any protection. He or she may be hassled because a younger brother or sister was seen hanging around. Picking on the younger kids is easier, though.

If that younger brother or sister has an older sibling doing something offensive, he or she may bear the brunt of it. Retaliation against a more vulnerable family member or even a friend is not unusual. Sometimes intercession helps, but not always. And if an ally turns to a gang, allegiance and loyalty can die in a minute.

You Gotta Know the Drill

That's why it doesn't pay to have too many friends. Knowing too much about someone else's business and letting a comment slip may result in being threatened or pushed around. It also doesn't pay to let someone else know your grades. Being smart is not cool in some circles, and that creates a target for someone who feels threatened by another's good grades.

Sometimes it's not what or who you know, but what you wear or don't wear that creates a climate for trouble. One common Catch-22 is in "matching" or not "matching." If the school has a certain dress code presumed by the student body (not the school) and someone departs from it, the oddball is at risk. If the sports jacket or athletic shoes are in, you're out if you don't have them. But if you do, you're at greater risk of being robbed and even killed for those clothes. What's wrong with this picture?

So what do you do to protect yourself at school when the standard daily fare is the presence of weapons and drugs, routine theft, and the regular threat of personal violence? You match and look good; act nice; blend in, don't be nosy; don't stare or make fun; don't talk about anyone and watch carefully what you say and do; keep your grades a secret; and tell the truth. If a teacher won't listen, tell the principal (and then watch out, just in case!)

That's Just in the City!

No it isn't. Jenna and Josie go to school in upstate New York, and Amy is in a smaller town in South Carolina. While this portrait of school is not the pattern of every school, it is not unique either. Many schools in rural or suburban areas are becoming just as dangerous as the stereotypical urban school. Perhaps the most remarkable thing about this report is that it describes the school culture of a magnet school; one of the best in a good school district. No wonder some of our students are afraid to go to school. Getting an education is a byproduct of daily survival.

For Further Reflection

Review the key points of this story by using the following discussion starters for conversation or reflection. The questions are asked of a school environment, but can also be applied to the community.

Good People and Bad People
■ Are there "good" people" and "bad" people at your school? How do you know who's who?

■ How do you get a bad reputation at your school? How do you keep a good reputation?

The Games We Play
■ What are the ways classmates interact, tease, torment, and support each other?

■ How does violent language (gossip, lies, half-truths, labels, slurs, and threats) affect the school population?

■ What positive "games" help maintain or work toward a good school climate?

"If You Touch Someone, They'll Beat You Up"
■ Are you afraid to go to school? Why or why not?

■ Are fights started for the fun of it? What can you do to protect yourself? others? to change that?

You Gotta Know the Drill
■ What do you do or not do to avoid trouble or fearful situations? What's the drill at your school?

■ Who can help in time of trouble? If there are no advocates or not enough, what can you do to find support?

Diana L. Hynson is an editor with The United Methodist Publishing House and has written and contributed to several youth publications including the series, Biblical Images for Today and To the Point: AIDS.

Violence as a Public Health Issue

by Todd Outcalt and Diana L. Hynson

Nicholas Elliot, then a sixteen-year-old student at the Atlantic Shores Christian School in Virginia Beach, Virginia, came to school on December 16, 1988 with a semi-automatic handgun hidden in his backpack. Nicholas had acquired the submachine gun, made specifically for close, military combat—a Cobray M-11/9—from a federally licensed dealer.

Later that morning, at the Christian school, Nicholas opened fire on several teachers, killing one while she sat in her office, and wounding another. Others teachers ran across the school yard, fleeing the bullets that the young man sprayed from his gun. Finally one man was able to tackle Nicholas and subdue him, saving a classroom of teenagers who were trapped at their desks. (Adapted from: Lethal Passage: *How the Travels of a Single Handgun Expose the Roots of America's Gun Crisis* by Eric Larson. To be published in March by Crown Publishers, Inc. Copyright © 1994 by Eric Larson. Based on an article that originally appeared in the ATLANTIC MONTHLY, January 1993.)

This story, not unlike so many others we read and hear about almost daily, is becoming one of the most deadly epidemics in our society. In a nation where our health care can prevent and treat nearly every kind of disease and illness, we have yet to curb the upswing of violence that is taking the lives of our teenagers at an alarming rate.

Consider that in the two years 1991 and 1992, there were 60,000 firearm deaths in the United States. This is more that the number of soldiers killed in the Vietnam War. Of that number, handguns account for 22,000 deaths. In 1991, in Los Angeles county alone, there were 8,050 persons killed or wounded. This is thirteen times the number of US casualties in the Persian Gulf War. And for every handgun used to kill someone, handguns also terrorize an alarming number of other kinds of victims DAILY. Assailants with handguns rape thirty-three women, rob 575 people, and assault another 1,116 *every day*. Among 11,000 surveyed teenagers in ten states, 41 percent of the boys and 21 percent of the girls said that they could get a handgun whenever they wanted.

More and more, teenagers are becoming at-risk for this type of violence, for a variety of reasons. Some will be perpetrators; others victims. A "none of my business" attitude about firearm production and distribution and a "make my day" attitude so prevalent in American culture, converge in a deadly mix. How bad does bad have to get before our society takes seriously this fatal threat?

A Vaccine for Violence?

We can prevent polio, typhoid, smallpox, and a host of other once deadly diseases with a simple childhood vaccine, but there is no vaccine or pill to cure violence. And yet violence is, more and more, being approached as a public health issue in an attempt to reverse it's spread.

Dr. Deborah Prothrow-Stith, physician and co-author of the book, *Deadly Consequences: How Violence Is Destroying Our Teenage Population and a Plan to Begin Solving the Problem*, has been speaking to this public health approach to violent behavior. She is convinced that our society must begin treating victims of violence as we would other types of at-risk patients. From personal experience and a host of other available statistics, she became aware that many of her patients had a greater risk of dying from a gunshot wound than they did of dying from cancer, heart disease, or AIDS. Now she has taken her public health approach to schools, churches, and conferences.

Homicide is now the leading cause of death among black teenage males—a rate seven times higher than among white teens of the same sex. And the incidents of shootings among both blacks and whites is most often perpetrated by friends or acquaintances of teenagers. This means that teens have a greater chance of being wounded or killed by a friend than they do a complete stranger on the street.

Dr. Prothrow-Stith addresses the public health approach to violence. She points out that solutions to this problem must embody multiple strategies and interventions.

Approaching violence as a public health issue involves so much more than creating catchy slogans like "Just say no," or handing out safety latches for guns. Prevention strategies are needed in families, schools, and communities that can target segments of the population that are at-risk, intervene with information and mutual networking, and then offer workable alternatives.

Mothers Against Drunk Driving (MADD) and SADD (for students) have had a profound effect on reducing drinking while driving, as have the American Heart Association and the American Cancer Association in their anti-smoking campaigns. More voluntary organizations will be needed to provide a support and educational network to combat violence.

Preventive Strategies

Most experts would agree that one primary avenue of stemming the tide of violence is through strengthening the family. Attorney General Janet Reno has been outspoken and continues to champion this cause. Workshops and training for parents, particularly single parent families, would be a step toward harmony. The church could take a more active role in providing STEP classes (Steps Toward Effective Parenting) and local YMCA's, YWCA's, and PTA's could make it a point to offer courses in schools dealing with effective parenting techniques.

Schools play a big role in forming our children's attitudes and beliefs. This is the location, other than home, where children spend the most amount of time. Although the schools are certainly overburdened with many other academic problems, our society needs to insure that every student has equal reinforcement and support from teachers and administrators. Relational skills might need to become a larger part of our effort, as well as teaching conflict management and helping kids to stay in school.

A community program could embody a prevention curriculum that would teach children and teenagers, especially inner city males, that they are at risk of becoming perpetrators or victims of violence and that they do have choices. No one has to be violent. There are alternatives.

For those at greatest risk, teens need to learn that when they spread rumors about other people, anger and mistrust continue to fester. More and more we are learning the wisdom of the adage: "Run away from a fight, not toward it." Angry arguments have a way of taking on more severe consequences. Incidents of name-calling and verbal abuse can lead to injury or death. More than this, many teens need to work toward overcoming some of their appetite for violence and thrills.

The best prevention strategy is always one that involves a variety of services, institutions, and individuals. It makes a difference when we see others around us as our neighbors and as those who may have fallen along the way and need our assistance.

Knowing the Odds

Whenever we read or hear about a murder in the paper or on television, we often make certain assumptions about the victim and the murderer. First we presume that the victim and assailant did not know each other. Perhaps we assume that the victim was "good" and the assailant was "bad," that they were of different races, and that the killing occurred during another type of crime. But the reality of death by homicide, including drug crimes, robbery, burglery, and other "stranger-bad guy stuff" as Dr. Prothrow-Stith calls it, accounts for about fifteen percent of violent deaths. Most homicides, *about sixty percent*, are committed by a family member, friend, or acquaintance. And the overwhelming majority of the time, nine

out of every ten murders, the assailant and victim are the same race.

What these facts tell us is that most murders are preventable. Most murders happen, not as a result of premeditated thought (or, in cold blood), but as a result of anger or uncontrolled feelings, and the handy availability of a gun. The vast majority of murders are hot blooded ones—the assailant doing little thinking, acting swiftly and recklessly.

Such findings make a compelling argument for gun control, but that is only part of the answer. Guns are not the only weapon in what Dr. Prothrow-Stith calls our national "make my day" ethic.

Drugs, alcohol, and poverty play their insidious part in creating a context of violence, but perhaps even more pervasive is something we can, but don't, control—anger. As Dr. Prothrow-Stith points out in *Deadly Consequences*, "One study of middle-class sons who became delinquent found that their parents had openly encouraged them to behave violently. These parents routinely threatened to punish their sons for not fighting; they advised them how to fight; they labelled not fighting as babyish and unmasculine; and they allowed fights to continue long after other parents would have intervened.

"As a physician I have been amazed by what parents teach their children about fighting. The mother of a teenage girl suspended from school after a fist fight applauded her child's action. 'Well, you wouldn't let someone call you names, would you?' she asked me. Even the most peaceful parents often feel compelled to goad their sons into aggressive behavior, fearing that a non-aggressive male must be a 'wimp.' 'Go out there and fight. Go out there and teach that so and so a lesson.' 'My parents will beat me unless I beat him,' is the way one young boy explained his parents' fighting philosophy to me.

"The result of parental indoctrination may be the creation of children who do not know how to cope with angry feelings in ways that are not violent." (Selected excerpts from *Deadly Consequences: How Violence is Destroying Our Teenage Population and a Plan to Begin Solving the Problem* by Deborah Prothrow-Stith M.D. and Michaele Weissman. Copyright © 1991 by Deborah Prothrow-Stith and Michaele Weissman. Reprinted by permission of HarperCollins Publishers, Inc.)

The "make my day" attitude is further reinforced and even lauded in the media as tough-guy "heroes" routinely blow away the bad guys, but for a good cause! And violence is not the sole province of males. More women are "modelling" violence, both as perpetrators and as those who are willing to use a weapon to retaliate against someone who "done them wrong." The standard fare for most made-for-TV movies seems to center chiefly around a few violent themes: revenge, stalking or terrorizing, rape, or violence to a child. Many schools continue the theme as students realize that in between lessons in survival, they are expected to get an education. (See the article "Living With Fear.")

Deborah Prothrow-Stith has made it a point to teach young people that violence will not go away by itself. We need to take an active role. Teens can help stem the tide of violence by learning nonaggressive ways to respond to violence, such as refusing to spread rumors and staying away from the scene of a fight—which merely adds incentive for the fight to continue. Teens can also work on their appetite for violence—they do not have to see movies that promote killing, for example. Avoiding violence is an important tactic, but perhaps the most critical lessons are those that promote active, intentional, nonviolence.

For Further Reflection

Consider Deborah Prothrow-Stith's approach to violence as a public health issue by using the following questions as discussion starters.

- Do you think violence is a public health issue? Why or why not? What specific ways do you think violence can be addressed as a health issue?
- Guns play a major role in death and injury of persons ages 15-24. What kind of public attitude can or should we have? What do you think about the availability of weapons? Would you own and/or use one? Why?
- What specific examples can you give of the "make my day" ethic? Do you think this is real? Do you think it has any effect on public and individual attitudes and participation in violence? Why or why not?

This Is Your Life . . . Not!

This activity looks at the effect labels have on how we regard ourselves and others.

As students arrive, tape labels on some persons' backs with titles like: *abuser, rapist, harasser, murderer*. On others give labels like: *loves children, kind to animals, loving, sympathetic*, and so forth. No one should know his or her own label.

☞ Ask everyone to mill around the room silently, taking note of the labels. After a few minutes invite students to form groups with those with whom they would like to be associated. Participants can move to and away from persons until you call time. The "violent" people will probably be ostracized.

☞ After groups have formed, have everyone reflect on their experiences by asking:

- How did it feel to be accepted? rejected?
- When were you first aware that others were cutting you off from the rest of the group?
- Why did you choose to cut others off from your group?

What About Your Health?

☞ Ask group members to brainstorm and list on newsprint as many types of violent behavior as they can. (Encour-

age a broad definition that goes beyond using weapons or overpowering with force, such as spreading rumors, lying, cheating.) Next allow the teens to define these behaviors, then discuss these questions.

- If you were the victim of any of these behaviors, how do you think it would affect your physical health? emotional health?

- Which of these behaviors do you do? Why? How do you think it affects others?

- Which would you never do? Why?

- In what situations do you see these behaviors? Are they done by people you admire? How do you feel and what do you think about that?

- What nonviolent options can you name for dealing with conflict? How can you practice them? teach them?

Look at How to "Make Your Day" With Nonviolence

Counteracting violence can be an overwhelming task that might make us feel defeated before we start. But handling the issue one step at a time makes the task less daunting and more manageable.

☞ Distribute news magazines or recent newspapers, scissors, and tape or pins. In groups of three, have participants make a montage of pictures and headlines that deal with violence.

☞ Select one or two specific headlines and ask the group to brainstorm all the barriers they can think of that keep us from overcoming that violence. Choose two or three barriers and begin to "peel" them, like an onion, working backward to identify some layer that you can address. Then work on an action plan to do it.

Their Day in Court

This exercise requires careful preparation with parents and community leaders, but can be influential.

☞ Invite local judges, lawyers, and law enforcement personnel to organize a mock trial and tour of the local jail facilities. Have one or two of your youth be "placed under arrest," led into the courtroom, and sentenced.

☞ The judge and lawyers can help to answer questions following the role playing. Afterwards, take your youth group to the county jail where they will be fingerprinted, photographed, and incarcerated until sentencing. Police officers can explain how our prison system operates.

Todd Outcalt is a United Methodist pastor in the South Indiana Conference. For the past five years he has taken youth on mission trips to Denver, Dallas, Canada, Milwaukee, and Louisiana. Todd lives in Indiana with his wife, Becky; daughter, Chelsey; and son, Logan.

A BRIEF HISTORY OF GUN CONTROL LEGISLATION

LAWS	EFFECT	OPPOSED BY
National Firearms Act, 1934	Taxed producers of machine guns, sawed-off shotguns, and so forth. Outlawed private possession of bombs, missiles, grenades, silencers.	Some manufacturers of arms
Gun Control Act of 1968	Changed the 1934 law, now making interstate sale of guns illegal. Guns could not be sold to minors or those with criminal records. Gunsellers had to be licensed and all sales transactions recorded.	Gunowners & NRA
Firearms Owners' Protection Act of 1986 (Gun Control Act)	Changed 1968 law after much lobbying. Permitted interstate sale of rifles & shotguns—not handguns. Dealers allowed to sell outside the store. Guns could now be purchased through mail.	Those wanting stricter gun control laws
Law Enforcement Officers Protection Act, 1985	Made illegal the production or importing of "vest piercing" bullets for handguns. Largely seen as a law to protect police.	Ammunition manufacturers & NRA
Brady Law, 1993	Instituted 7 day waiting period on new gun purchases, allowing police to check records of buyer's criminal record and history.	NRA

*Note: In addition to these federal laws there are a host of State and local laws. Some states, in response to various federal regulations, have made handgun possession unrestricted. Other states (and some towns) have banned handgun sales and placed restrictions on gun use. Readers should consult their own state laws governing the use of handguns.

**These facts were taken from: *Gun Control,* An American Issue, Information Plus, © 1991 Edition. Mark Siegal, Editor

GUNS AND PUBLIC HEALTH

The medical community has begun to address gun violence with the same urgency as any dreaded disease. Gun-related statistics are heightening our awareness of how gun violence affects many aspects of our health care. Consider the following information quoted from *Gun Control,* by David Newton, Enslow Publishers, 1992:

* On average, a person is killed or wounded by a gun every 2.5 minutes in the United States (page 7).

* Guns now account for 10 percent of all childhood deaths between the ages of one and nineteen (page 7).

* In 1989, 1,897 children under the age of sixteen were killed by firearms (page 7).

* The economic costs of gunshot injuries is staggering. During the years 1987 and 1988, Highland Hospital in Oakland, California treated about 700 gunshot victims at a total health care cost of $10.5 million, with these patients using 40% of the blood supply (page 103).

* The nationwide cost for treating gunshot victims has now reached $1 billion annually, with taxpayers covering 85 percent of the costs (page 103).

Ritual Abuse

by Beth A. Richardson

Words of Caution

Ritual abuse is dangerous. It is not a topic that can be covered adequately in a few pages. Nor is it a subject to be raised with youth if you are not trained to do so. If you have any questions, ask for help. Use these pages to introduce yourself to the topic so that you can begin to be an advocate for teens at risk of ritual abuse. See the section "Where to Go for Help" on pages 90-94.)

Why Talk About This?

Ritual abuse is an area of emerging knowledge. This type of abuse has been around for a long time, but it has only been named and discussed in public arenas in recent years.

Ritual abuse is often sensationalized in the media and discounted as the claims of disturbed people or the isolated activity of a few. But ritual abuse is real. It happens more frequently than any of us would like to think. In a 1991 survey of 2,709 psychologists, 30% reported having seen at least one case of ritual/religious abuse. A total of 5,731 ritual/religious abuse cases were reported. (From "Profile of Ritualistic and Religion-Related Abuse Allegations Reported to Clinical Psychologists in the United States" by Bette L. Bottoms, et al. Presented at American Psychological Association, San Francisco CA, August, 1991.)

Youth are especially vulnerable to being drawn into ritual abuse settings. Teens are establishing their own identities, separate from family and church. This openness to new things, coupled with lesser power (in relation to adults), makes them vulnerable to groups that recruit youth in order to take advantage of them.

Educate yourself about ritual abuse and learn to recognize its signs and symptoms.

What Is Ritual Abuse?

According to David W. Lloyd, J.D., ritualistic victimization is "the intentional, repeated, and stylized psychological abuse of a child accompanied by criminal acts directed against the child, typified by physical assault and sexual victimization of the child, cruelty to animals, or threats of harm to the child, other persons, and animals." (From *RoundTable* [Spring 1992] by David Lloyd. Page 17.)

Ritual abuse is characterized by unbelievable violence and unspeakable, heinous acts. Survivors of ritual abuse tell of ritualized gang rape, mutilation of animals and humans, murder, witnessing or participating in human (often infant) sacrifice, eating feces or human flesh, and mind control techniques utilizing threats and electric shock. Ritual abuse is most often associated with abuse by satanic cults. But ritual abuse may also be perpetrated by religious cults, secret societies such as the KKK, politically based groups such as organized crime, or by individuals and families. (From "Ritual Abuse: A More Accurate Language and Its Implications" by Elizabeth Power. [MPD/DD Resource and Education Center, Nashville, TN.] Page 2)

Because of the nature of the abuse and the level of violence, suspicion of ritual abuse should be referred to professionals who can help. Do not try to handle this by yourself.

Hadley's Story

Hadley is fourteen. Her father is a doctor, her mother a teacher. She has a younger brother and sister. Hadley plays trumpet in the concert band and is a member of the girl's soccer team. She makes mostly B's and some A's in school. Her friends like her a lot, even though she is kind of shy.

Hadley's family has gone to church forever. Her parents were raised in the church. Hadley and her sister and brother were all baptized when they were babies. The whole family goes to church every Sunday and Hadley is in the junior high youth fellowship group.

Hadley's family also has another activity. But the people at church don't know about it. Neither do Hadley's friends or teachers. Hadley can't remember a time when it wasn't happening. Whenever her parents take her, she usually gets some kind of shot or has to take a pill. It happens mostly at night and sometimes it's hard for her to remember it. But she knows that she always feels awful and sometimes her body hurts for a long time afterwards. She sees things that are really bad, worse than on TV. Sometimes there is a lot of blood. Most of the time, she gets raped. And she has been told and she believes that if she ever tells anyone, her younger brother or sister will be hurt.

Hadley likes to go to church, but she gets really confused about what they say there — "Don't commit adultery." "Love the Lord your God." "Don't kill." "Jesus loves the little children."

Hadley is afraid of what the people at church would think of the things she and her family do in the night.

And she decided years ago that God hates her. But sometimes, when she hears about God loving people, she wishes it could be true for her, too.

Ritual Abuse Challenges Our World View

When we hear about ritual abuse, we hear about satanic rituals, orgies, sacrifice, and torture. These stories do not fit into our theology and our world view. We are profoundly changed when we learn about such cruelty and evil. Just hearing about ritual abuse brings us face to face with questions about human nature, about God's participation in the world, and about the presence of evil.

Ritual abuse is controversial. A societal denial tries to suppress knowledge of ritual abuse. We cannot see what we do not believe. And as people of faith, we want to believe that these kinds of things do not happen, especially to people in our churches. We do not want to believe that people like us are capable of committing acts of such cruelty, particularly against children.

It has always been difficult for our culture to accept the truth about acts of violence. In the 1890's, Sigmund Freud documented cases of father-daughter incest. After his initial findings were reported, he was publicly challenged by colleagues who did not believe that incest happened. Freud later recanted his findings. He wrote that he must have been wrong because "it was hardly credible that perverted acts against children were so general." (From *The Origins of Psychoanalysis: Letters to Wilhelm Fliess,* Drafts and Notes: 1887-1902 by Sigmund Freud. New York Basic Books, 1954, page 215.) Since that time, the existence of sexual abuse has been alternately "discovered" and suppressed about every 35 years. (From *Psychiatric Clinics of North America* Vol. 12 No. 2, "The Centrality of Victimization" by Roland C. Summit. June 1989, page 413.)

During World War II, stories were coming out of Germany and Poland about mass murder in the Nazi death camps. But world leaders did not believe the reports because they were too terrible. A 1993 survey found that one in five Americans (22%) believes it is possible that the Holocaust never happened. (Roper Organization survey cited in "Holocaust Museum Sends Message to Doubters" by Ray Waddle. [printed in *The Tennessean* April 22, 1993.)] And that is with the evidence we have access to — the pictures, stories of survivors, and detailed record-keeping from the Nazis themselves.

But we as a faith community have an opportunity to witness to the truth that ritual abuse happens and to say no to the violence. The abuse cannot be stopped if people don't believe that it is true. We have a special responsibility to guide our youth to a spirituality that stands for wholeness and life rather than violence and death.

Youth at Risk

Teens may be victims of ritual abuse in at least two ways—they may be exposed to it through the involvement of their family. Or they may be recruited by groups involved in ritual abuse.

In situations of familial ritual abuse, youth have probably been exposed to abuse for a long time. Teens growing up in violent families adapt to the abuse because they have few other options for survival. They may appear as "normal" as teens from healthy homes. But often they will exhibit symptoms of abuse: age-inappropriate sexual knowledge or behavior, severe emotional or behavioral problems, eating disorders, or addictions. These symptoms are the same for a variety of problems, so it is important to refer youth to qualified professionals for evaluation and treatment.

Teens are also at risk for recruitment to groups that perpetrate ritual abuse. They are vulnerable in their search for their own, separate identity. Groups such as cults intentionally seek out youth because of these vulnerabilities. A 1992 survey of former cult members reported that ten percent were in high school when they were recruited by their cult. (International Cult Education Program, PO Box 1232, Gracie Station, New York, NY 10028.) Teens are promised spiritual fulfillment, financial success, and community. Groups associated with Satanism lure youth with promises of money, power, sex, and drugs.

Signs and Symptoms

Watch for these signs and symptoms. (Remember that these can indicate a number of problems, so don't over-react.)

▶ *Sudden changes in behavior, school involvement, grades*

▶ *Increased drug or alcohol use or acting out behavior*

▶ *Intense interest in the occult, occult symbols, and occult values*

▶ *Alienation from family and religion*

▶ *Unusual activity around satanic holidays, full moons, the solstice or equinox*

▶ *Self-mutilating behavior*

▶ *Scars or bruises*

What Can We Do?

Don't wait until you suspect ritual abuse to get ready. Plan ahead. Here are some things you can do to be prepared.

▶ **Educate yourself and other adult friends of teens.** Ritual abuse is complicated and hard to hear about. It's difficult to help someone else if you have not worked through your feelings about something. See page 95 to find other materials. Read and discuss what you find with other adults. See the sections "When Someone Comes to You" and "Legal Knowledge Is Key."

▶ **Identify professionals** who can receive referrals and develop a relationship with them. Find professionals who have worked with cases of ritual abuse and who believe that it happens. (Even professionals can deny the reality of ritual abuse.) Identify supportive mental health persons, social workers, and law enforcement personnel. Develop a working relationship with them.

▶ **Make a plan for dealing with disclosures.** Coordinate the plan with other adult workers with youth. Write down the steps you would follow if you suspected ritual abuse or received a disclosure.

▶ **Refer.** If you receive a disclosure or suspect ritual abuse is happening, don't try to handle it alone. Call in professional help.

▶ **Care for the caregiver.** Stay grounded in your faith. Ritual abuse is difficult for both the victims and those who care for them. Learning about ritual abuse is a life-changing event. Know ahead of time that it is a difficult subject to read and talk about. Talk with others about what you are learning. Spend time in prayer and rest in God.

▶ **Care for the victim.** Above all, believe the teen who trusts you with a disclosure. Listen; acknowledge that you have heard. Be present in compassion. (Compassion means to suffer with.) Do not ask, "Are you sure?" Treat the disclosure as truth and refer to a professional. Be open to hearing difficult questions about God and feelings of anger and betrayal. These feelings are a normal part of the hurt and the healing. Continue to provide support for the teen throughout the process. Remember that if the abuse has occurred in a religious context, traditional "God talk" will not be comforting and may alienate. If you are unable to provide ongoing support, find someone else who can be there for the teen.

▶ **Know that healing takes a long time.** The teen will be hurting long after you are ready for it to be all over. Do not push the need to forgive and forget prematurely. Be patient and supportive.

David's Story

David is a junior in high school. He's always had an interest in old stuff — Medieval culture, druids. He's been into "Dungeons and Dragons"™ since he was in third grade. He's had lots of conversations with his Sunday school teacher about other types of spirituality, and he really likes some of their ideas — protecting the earth, the connection of all living things, and so forth.

So David was pumped up about going to a party with a new friend of his. They met at school and hit it off right away. His friend was into some of the same stuff that he was, and he told David about a group where he could learn lots about the old ways.

Early one Saturday night, David went to his friend's house and they rode with some older teens out into the countryside. When they arrived, there were lots of people there. There was a fire in the middle of a field, and most of the people were dressed in robes. David was fascinated by the ritual and the strange words. But then he started feeling scared when he saw some little kids who were tied up.

David wished that he hadn't come. He wanted to leave, but he was afraid of looking stupid. Besides, he couldn't walk all the way home. Sometime in the night, an older man came up to David and showed him a picture. It was David's mom getting out of her car at the grocery store. The man said that he hoped David would come back again. And he said that if David ever told anything about that night, they would kill his mother. David broke out in a sweat and wondered what in the world he should do.

About Prevention

Prevention of ritual abuse involves helping youth develop and maintain a solid basis of community, values, and spirituality. Here are some things you can do to nurture these strengths.

▶ **Help youth maintain links with the community of faith.** Who are adults that they feel they could tell if something bad was happening to them? What makes that adult someone they could trust? If there is no one, what qualities would it take for that trust to happen?

▶ **Help youth define their values.** What's okay and what's not? Why? What things do they see on TV or in the movies that are okay? not okay? (See the section on "Media.") Are there ever promises that should not be kept? Which ones?

▶ **Help youth explore their Christian faith.** What do teens value about their Christian faith? What do they find missing in the Christian faith? What is attractive in alternate forms of spirituality? Why? What is missing in alternate forms of spirituality? Keep the discussion alive. Listen, be interested in what is said, and affirm the searching that you are hearing without trying to come to a neat solution.

For Further Reflection

Theological Reflection

The Holocaust changed the way that people of the Jewish faith view the world and God. Reflect on the ways that you as a member of the community of faith are affected by such abject evil as ritual abuse.

■ Has learning about ritual abuse changed the way you think about the world, God, evil, or human beings? If so, how?

■ What are ways that God is at work (or not at work) in relation to ritual abuse?

■ Read these Scriptures of hope: **Psalm 27** (see especially verse 10 in *Today's English Version*) and **Psalm 139:7-12**. Make a list of promises of hope that you hold inside of you (from Scripture, nature, friends, or your faith community). What words of hope could you offer to one without hope?

Roleplay a Disclosure About Ritual Abuse

☞ Ask for two volunteers to act out a scene in which one tells the other about abuse. Use either Hadley or David's story as a starting point, or make up your own situation. In this situation, it would probably be best for an adult to model first the role of the listener.

■ What do you say to him or her?

■ What actions do you take following the disclosure? See "Legal Knowledge is Key" page 12.

■ What feelings do you have about dealing with the situation?

Biblical Reflection on Luke 15:11-31

Survivors of ritual abuse are often taught that they are unacceptable to any person or to God.

☞ Read **Luke 15:11-31**, the story of the prodigal child and the loving parent and discuss these questions.

■ "No matter what happens to you, no matter who you are, no matter what you have done, God loves you and accepts you." Do you think this statement is true or false? Why?

■ The younger child chose to come home even though he had done some things his father would not like. Have you ever done something that made you wish you would not have to go home? Is there any act you can think of that would make you not come home to your parents? to God?

■ If you were God, what would you say to someone who felt he or she could not come home?

Beth A. Richardson is a United Methodist diaconal minister and assistant editor of alive now! *magazine. She is a writer, educator, and consultant on issues of abuse.*

I Regret What I Have Done

by Mark Anderson

I Used to Have a Normal Life

I was a five year old boy with a normal life and normal parents. The summer before my kindergarten year many things changed and affected me forever. My biological father sexually abused me. He forced me to perform oral sex with him five times and five times it was branded on my brain. I was scared of my parents, especially my father. I would cry very easily to get other people's attention. When my parents were not around, I acted tough so people wouldn't bother me. I carried this anger with me until after my parents got a divorce.

But It Didn't Last Long

When I was about eleven years old, I started to abuse my two-year-old sister. I got caught quickly, but my mother passed it off as curiosity. When I was fifteen I perpetrated again, this time against my five-year-old sister. Again I was caught quickly. This time my mother sent me to an evaluation hospital in Texas. After I got out of the hospital, I went through eighteen months of therapy.

I was seventeen-years-old when I abused my seven- and five-year-old sisters. My mother called the sheriff's department to pick me up and put me in juvenile detention to protect my little sisters.

I was charged with three counts of aggravated rape against my seven-year-old sister. I fondled, digitally penetrated, and performed oral sex on her. I was also charged with two counts of sexual battery against my five-year-old sister. I touched the outside of her genital area with her clothes on.

Afterwards I was committed to a youth detention facility by the court. I got the chance that I will not get when I am an adult, if I do this again. I was sent to a treatment center, which is where I am right now.

The Emotional Fallout

My mother was quite angry with my action towards my sisters, but she told me she still loves me. I had a normal life before I got locked up. I had a girlfriend, went to school, and played sports. Now all that has changed. I will never be fully trusted around little kids. That is a scary thought considering I might have kids of my own some day.

In my adult life I will be labeled a sexual perpetrator. I am not looking forward to that. So I am getting help now. That will bother me for a long time to come, as much as it will bother other people. My siblings will think of me differently. My sisters are scared of me. I have scarred them as I was scarred as a kid.

I hate my biological father for what he did, but I love him for being my father. He was a good man with one bad fault—sexual abuse. I have forgiven him for what he has done, and I hope my sisters forgive me for what I have done.

What Does the Future Hold?

Why did I do it? The doctors say that most perpetrators have been victimized. Well that was not the only reason. I was also inhaling Scotch Guard and Suede cleaner. I was hallucinating that I was in my father's position. I regret doing what I have done, but the past is unchangeable. I need to worry about the future and my children, if I decide to have children.

For Further Reflection

Explore some of the key points in Mark's story by using these discussion starters.

"I Had a Normal Life"

Twice Mark says he had a normal life—before he was abused and before he was locked up.

■ How is Mark defining normal? How would you define it? If there is a difference, how do you explain it?

■ When your life feels crazy what do you do to find something normal or familiar?

"My Mother Caught Me"

■ What did Mark's mother do? What do you think you would do? Why?

■ What was her response to what Mark has done? How do you think you would feel? Why?

"I Will Never Be Fully Trusted"

There is no cure for pedophilia; only treatment. Mark knows he and his sisters have been hurt deeply by the family's abusive pattern.

■ What kind of life do you think Mark can expect?

■ What might Mark (or Mark's family) have done or not done to change things?

■ What place does forgiveness have in this family story?

Mark Anderson (not his real name) is a teen currently in treatment in a Southern hospital that specializes in the care of troubled youth. Mark has told his story in the hope that it will help someone else.

Dealing With Severe Trauma and Tragedy

by Jeffrey Skinner

Trauma and Adolescents

By the time you reach the age of 15 or 16, it is likely that you will know someone who has experienced a trauma. Victims of trauma are no different than you and your friends. We rely on the trust of others to get most of our personal needs met. That trust is broken when we are victimized.

The death of a pet and the ensuing grief at age seven can be eased by the empathy of parents. Our hurt can be patched. However, the protective shield that parents once provided can no longer extend its same protection during adolescence. It is estimated that the deaths of most adolescents happen as a result of accidents and, next, as a result of suicide. As parents once helped the eight-year-old be safe and protected that child from harm and trauma, the adolescent now must learn how to keep himself or herself safe. He or she must rely more on his or her own coping mechanisms in dealing with his or her emotional and intellectual responses to severe trauma and tragedy.

Tragedies are something that we can all expect to experience, such as the death of a pet. Severe traumas are experiences that are not in the usual course of everyday human experience, for example, suicide; death of a parent; sexual abuse; physical abuse; attacks; rape (male and female); witnessing a shooting, robbery, or kidnapping.

Many adolescents believe they are exempt from being the victims of trauma. Too often, they tell their parents that, "I know how to take care of myself." When a parent asks the teen for more details, he or she usually says, "Don't you trust me and my judgment?" The self-proclaimed good judgment of a teenager reflects the increased and enjoyed power of greater analytical thinking. Adolescents are at high risk for experiencing traumas as a result of omnipotent thinking, which is, "I know how to take care of myself; nothing bad will happen to me." The reality is that victims of rape, shootings, natural disasters, catastrophes, and so forth are people like us and our friends.

> *Adolescents are at high risk for experiencing traumas as a result of omnipotent thinking, which is, "I know how to take care of myself; nothing bad will happen to me."*

Coping with Trauma and Tragedy

The experience of loss is at the core of the effects of trauma and tragedy. The loss of a grandparent or a pet is expressed through grieving, which is a normal response to tragedy. Grieving involves a mixture of emotions that come and go. Profound sadness, loneliness, anger, disbelief, denial, and pessimism are usually experienced. Acceptance of the loss happens, after time, with a more optimistic sense of the future.

Coping with severe trauma is something like grieving the loss in a tragedy, except that witnessing a trauma, or being the victim of trauma, can actually threaten the life and future well-being of the person. Denial, shock, terror, and retreat into the self are usually the first responses to trauma. Physical responses of shaking, vomiting, and feeling hysterical are also common. Adolescents who witness a suicide, or are a friend of the victim, just "can't believe" something like this could happen. In time, those teens will be able to express anger and resentment toward the peer who committed suicide.

David and Jack

Jack's best friend, David, killed himself with his father's shotgun when his application to a prestigious college was rejected. David personally felt rejected and never let his parents really know how he felt. David always felt pressured by his parents and eventually placed unreachable expectations on himself. Jack was with David the afternoon prior to David's committing suicide. When Jack received the alarming phone call from David's parents, Jack was shocked, and felt like someone was playing a trick on him. That night Jack could not sleep; he cried to himself and longed to go to David's house to really see for himself. For several days, Jack felt numb and sad—as if he couldn't have any of his usual feelings. Through discussions with parents and friends, Jack later accepted the reality of his friend's death. He expressed resentment that he and David wouldn't be able to grow up together. Jack knew that he would always carry the loss of his friend with him for the remainder of his life.

Trauma inflicted through rape, sexual abuse, and physical abuse can be devastating, especially if the teen keeps feelings and thoughts bottled up. If such trauma happens before adolescence, it is likely that the child may have felt he or she deserved it or caused the abuse.

Often, adolescence marks the time when people first disclose childhood trauma, as the youth sees that he or she was not to blame. Many adolescents stay in denial of their feelings until they realize that being a victim of trauma may not always mean they are to blame. "Saving face" at the expense of telling others, especially adults, is a method of coping and allows the teen to gain control of his or her profound feelings. Loss of control over oneself and one's environment is a major threat for adolescents who are just beginning to master self-control.

Unfortunately, trauma experienced through date rape often goes unreported as victims have many reasons not to heighten their trauma in an unwitnessed crime. The following vignette illustrates this point and others.

Lisa's Blind Date

Lisa had a blind date set up through a friend. After the movie, they went to eat, and somehow, they ended up at the house of another friend. Lisa felt pressured by her date for sexual activity, which she was not really anticipating. Before she could stop her date, he overpowered her, raped her, and told her never to tell or he would tell all her friends that she was a prostitute. Lisa was left there by her date, and her girlfriends took her home. She told only one girlfriend and hid everything else from her parents. That night, she cried herself to sleep, threw her clothes away, and felt that if her parents knew, she would be grounded for life. For several days, she did not go to school, and she avoided contact with her family. Lisa developed a fear of cars similar to her date's car. She later decided that she would always look sloppy so no one would ever ask her out on a date again. Through several months of depression, finally Lisa told her mother about the trauma. Healing then began, but not without painful feelings.

Signs of Difficulty in Coping

Responses to trauma and resulting, long-lasting (one month or more) symptoms are common. Many soldiers and war veterans, victims of rape and tragedy report the following symptoms:

▶ nightmares

▶ avoiding situations that remind one of the trauma

▶ fear

▶ withdrawal, feeling numb, or depression

▶ poor concentration

▶ feeling detached; feeling that things don't seem real

▶ flashbacks

▶ pessimism about the future

The major consequence of not dealing with the thoughts and feelings of the trauma is a diminishing sense of self-competency and a likelihood of remaining vulnerable to ordinary stress. Further, if sexually traumatized, one may later feel insecure about one's sexual life and may choose repetitive harmful relationships in the future. If you or others are worried about someone, talk to them, your pastor, church leader, or your parents. A referral to a mental health professional may be indicated.

Teens Helping Teens

Teen peers seem to be the first ones to talk to each other, as intimacy and trust are usually sought in peer relations. In dealing with a friend who has experienced severe trauma, it is important not to make value judgments, but rather to be accepting of the feelings, which may also be scary. Be supportive and listen for ways you may increase the self-esteem of the traumatized peer.

If a peer is talking about suicide, do not make promises that you will not tell an adult. Often in schools, if one student has killed himself or herself, others may copycat or mimic a suicide attempt. Encourage and solicit a conversation among caring adults and teens if a suicide has occurred at your school, church, or in your community.

Adults Helping Teens in Trauma

Children and youth who have experienced trauma at the hands of an adult may be very mistrusting of adults. It is common for people who have been sexually or physically abused to assume a hyper-vigilant posture. Such teens need a sense of safety and security from other adults. Forming a close, intimate relationship may, at first, be frightening for a victimized teen. Take time to develop a secure, safe relationship, built first upon respect. In time, closeness will develop, only after the adolescent can sense that his or her judgment about your intentions is sound and not exploitative. (See the article "Being Pastoral" on page 6.)

Physically and sexually traumatized teens, who have been harmed by family members, experience conflict in loyalty to their family and to others outside. Ambivalence in love is to be recognized and validated. Advocating for traumatized youth helps the youth feel supported. If legal and government processes are involved, recognize that the teen has many pressures placed upon him or her. Advocates should be well informed and be sensitive to the multiple systems.

The Christian Response

Historically, the church has missions to both transform systems and to serve others. For example, opportunities in local churches may exist to examine and challenge the programs schools offer to respond to teen suicide. Some churches are active in changing systems that recognize the need for improved services for victims of trauma, especially human-induced trauma. The church may have a role in surveying services in the community for traumatized youth or ensuring that services are responsive to current needs.

Service to others can encompass sensitizing church leaders in the dynamics of trauma and ways youths cope. Opportunities may exist for the establishment of a support group for severely abused girls or boys or a support group for teenagers who have been raped. Some churches may collaborate with a local pastoral counseling center to develop a trauma debriefing team. Such a team, comprised of lay leaders and professional mental health providers, could help a teen and family process the trauma and then reduce the likelihood of post-trauma difficulties.

For Further Reflection

Review the Terms and Signs

■ What is the difference between a trauma and a tragedy?

■ What are some signs that indicate a person has experienced a trauma or tragedy?

■ What are some of the ways we cope with tragedy?

■ What is one significant reason that teens are at risk of trauma or tragedy?

Think About the People You Know

Think to yourself about any adolescent or peer you know who has experienced trauma. Not everyone will develop dysfunctional methods of coping with trauma.

■ After reading the article, do you recall anything about that person's experience (or your own) that you overlooked before, such as realizing a certain level of denial?

■ What are some ways you can extend help? What are some things you should not do?

■ Why do you think some people may develop symptoms that require treatment from a professional?
If you think you or someone you know needs professional help, what can you do? What should you not do?

Investigate Words of the Faith

Often times, when trauma or tragedy occurs, people experience a crisis in their faith and feel that they are losing their faith. The theological concepts of "evil" and "good" are complex and can become more complicated for a victim of trauma.

☞ Have Bibles and commentaries handy to consider these questions and Scriptures.

■ If we lose trust in others, how might this affect our trust in God?

■ Does the meaning of our world, our life, or the life of our friends change once we have experienced trauma or tragedy? If so, how?

☞ Ask **older youth** to read **Psalms 22** and **23** and ask the following questions.

■ What do these psalms reveal about the character of God? What are your clues?

■ What do these psalms reveal about the person praying? What are your clues?

■ Do you think God causes tragedy? Why or why not?

☞ Ask **younger youth** to read **Lamentations 3:31-33** and **John 10:7-11** and ask these questions.

■ What do you think these Scriptures say about God? about people? Why?

■ Do you think bad things just happen or does God cause them to happen? Why do you think so?

☞ After you have discussed the questions, write a pastoral prayer that reflects your thoughts and what you perceive as God's love. Consider writing a group prayer and asking your pastor, liturgist, or worship leaders if it may be used during worship service.

Practice Giving Support

☞ Form two groups to roleplay. Use either the story about Jack and David or about Lisa. (You may photocopy them.) Set up the roleplay between the teen and an adult or another teen who is attempting to help. Everyone can take turns playing different roles to see what it feels like.

☞ Process the experience in a large group format by asking these questions.

■ Is there a stigma associated with being a victim? If so, what might it be?

■ What did you say or do that was helpful? That was not helpful? What would you do differently?

■ How can Christians help destigmatize victims of tragedy or trauma?

■ What feelings do you think someone might have who has been raped or severely assaulted? What purpose do these feelings play in helping the person maintain his or her psychological equilibrium?

■ Why might some adolescents be reluctant to describe feelings to an adult about a personal trauma? How can trust be redeveloped?

■ What would be your statement to someone who said he or she was abused as an eight-year-old?

Take a "Safety Inventory" of Your Church

■ Do you feel your church is safe from rapists, muggers, or those who would inflict bodily harm? What awareness do church leaders have about this?

■ What do we do with our discomfort if we must develop a protective shield around our church?

■ Do you feel your church community can address issues of trauma? Why or why not?

■ What changes or improvements must your church make to offer a caring ministry for traumatized persons? How can you work toward that?

Jeff Skinner, M.Div. LCSW, is a psychotherapist in Nashville, TN who specializes in treating adolescents and their families.

An Inside Look at Gangs

by Jacob Smith as told to Gail Bock

An Inside Look at Gangs

Jacob Smith of Queen's, New York is a twenty-three-year-old former Hard Core Street Youth. He spent years on the street engaging in gang type activities, but did not actually join a gang. Jacob didn't care about gang affiliation because he could make more money on his own. He does however know many, many gang members from the time he spent on the streets.

Jacob gave up the street life because he got tired of running, spending time in jail, and being assaulted by other street youth.

He is now active in a National Leadership organization called Outward Bound. Outward Bound works with youth from local high schools in community building, ethnic community building, and personal building. Jacob is also a member of Children of War, an International Youth Organization that promotes the healing process through sharing personal stories of war and violence. Members of Children of War go into the community and do positive things to benefit the community, like becoming involved in Outward Bound and other outreach groups.

Here, Jacob talks to us about life on the streets and about gangs.

Gangs, Posses, and Street Youth

There are four different types of youth who live on and work the streets.

Gangs seem to be fairly structured. Some gangs have ceremonies for initiation into the group and other occasions. Gangs may also have governing rules, such as "Don't trespass into another gang's territory," or "Don't talk to a fellow gangster's girl."

Posses are an unstructured group of youth, like a street clique. They are similar to gangs in appearance and actions but they don't have set rules that govern the group. The only unwritten rule the Posse follows is to look out for each other.

Regular Street Youth do minimal negative activities and go home at night.

Hard Core Street Youth participate in maximum negative activities, such as hustling money playing craps, cards, hoops, and skelly (a game played with a top). Additional negative activities include burglary, car theft, and holdups. They are on the street and engage in negative activities twenty-four hours a day, seven days a week.

Gang Appeal

Youth join gangs for a sense of family they don't get at home. They feel like they get the love, care, and security from the gang that they do not get from parents or guardians. Gang members can "act out" in gangs and not be looked upon as being bad. Acting out behaviors include swearing at your girl, at those who stare at you, or other gang members; disrespecting your girl; acting like you don't care about anything; daring someone to kill you if you feel like you've been "dissed"; stealing; and going to jail. (Serving jail time makes the "jailer a big guy.") Sometimes kids join, not because of what they are missing at home, but out of curiosity, and once they get in they have a hard time getting out.

The Underside of Belonging

Once you get into a gang it's hard to get out. Your life expectancy drops. Jacob reports: "They (gang members) don't expect to see next year, or up to their 21st year. You'd be lucky to see your 22nd, 23rd, or 24th birthday, and even then you still ain't looking at 25."

How Do Gang Members Respond to Violence?

Gang members respond to violence with violence. "Gangsters can't be looked upon as being weak. They gotta get theirs back."

Ex-gang Members Respond to Violence

It's hard to change one's responses. The ex-gang member must realize that the conflict is symptomatic of deeper feelings. They have to determine what these feelings are. It takes a lot of time and work not to respond in kind.

The Greatest Fear

Oddly enough, dying is not the answer. Losing power to anyone—another gang member or to other gangs—is a gangster's greatest fear.

Faith, Religion, and the Church

What do faith, religion, and the church offer to gang members? Jacobs' response: "In my experience, nothing. Churches don't seek out gang members. And gang members don't seek out the church; it is a sign of weakness. Rarely, a gang member or two may gravitate back to the church but they don't broadcast that fact to fellow gang members." (Because they don't want to be thought of as weak by their peers.)

Who Can Help?

It would be hard for adults to tell if a family member was involved in a gang. Signs that may indicate gang affiliation may include a tattoo, the way a hat or pair of pants is worn, or a brand of tennis shoe that is worn. But on the other hand, none of these things may indicate gang affiliation; it may just be a phase your youth is going through. If you are positive your child has joined a gang, try giving him or her the things he or she is getting from the gang: understanding, love, care, and a sense of security. If your child doesn't want out, there is not a lot you can do, but be there to support and love him or her in whatever decision he or she makes.

● ●

Life on the Street

In this heightened atmosphere of violence [on the street], normal rules of behavior don't apply. As traditional social supports—home, school, community—have fallen away, new role models have taken their place. "It takes an entire village to raise a child, but the village isn't there for the children anymore," says Jeff Modisett, the Indianapolis prosecutor. "The only direction these kids receive is from their peers on the street, the local drug dealers and other role models who engage in criminal conduct." Katie Buckland, a Los Angeles prosecutor who volunteers in the city's schools, says the kids she sees have already given up the idea of conventional success and seize the opportunities available. "The kids that are selling crack when they're in the fifth grade are not the dumb kids," she says. "They're the smart kids. They're the ambitious kids . . . trying to climb up their own corporate ladder. And the only corporate ladder they see has to do with gangs and drugs."

With drugs the easy route to easy money, prison is the dominant institution shaping culture, replacing church and school. In the last few years, more young black men have gone to jail than to college. Fathers, uncles, brothers, cousins have all done time. April Allen, a 15-year-old who lives in Boston's Roxbury section, has friends who think of jail as a kind of sleep-away camp. "The boys I know think it's fun to be in jail because other boys they know are in jail, too," she says. Prison is a way of looking: the dropped waist, baggy-pants look is even called "jailing" in Miami. And prison is a way of acting. "In prison, the baddest, meanest guy runs the cell," says H.T. Smith, a lawyer and African-American activist who practices in Miami's Overtown ghetto. "Your neighborhood, your school—it's the same. You've got to show him you're crazy enough so he won't mess with you."

If prison provides the method of social interaction, guns provide the means . . .

One kid with a gun is a finite danger; a gang equipped with Uzis, AK-47s and sawed-off shotguns means carnage. Unlike adult criminals, who usually act alone, violent teens normally move in a pack. That's typical teen behavior: hanging together. But these are well-equipped armies, not just a few kids milling outside a pizza parlor. There's a synergistic effect: one particularly aggressive kid can spur others to commit crimes they might not think of on their own. The victims are often chosen because they are perceived as weak or vulnerable, say social scientists who study children and aggression. As horrible as some of the crimes are, kids go along with the crowd rather than go it alone.

Risk Factors

After a while, life on the streets begins to feel like home to older teenagers. Joachin Ramos, a 19-year-old member of the Latin Counts in Detroit, says he spends his time "chillin' and hanging" with the Counts when he's not in jail. He's spent two years behind bars, but that hasn't made him turn away from the gang. The oldest of seven children, he never met his father, but he has been told that he was a member of the Bagly Boys, a popular gang a generation ago. Ramos began carrying a gun when we was 9; he became a full-fledged Count at the age of 13. He has watched three good friends—Bootis, Shadow, and Showtime—die in street wars.

Some kids do manage to leave street life, usually with the help of a supportive adult. William Jefferson, now 19, quit the Intervale gang in Boston's Roxbury section after he was shot. "My mom talked to me and told me I had to make a decision whether I wanted to do something with my life or stay on the street and possibly get killed." He started playing basketball and football at school; then he had to keep up his grades to stay on the teams. Last month he became the first of his mother's four children to graduate from high school. He plans to enter junior college this fall. Now, he says, he'll behave because "I have a lot to lose."

Girls Will Be Girls

Girls are breaking into the traditionally male world of gangs, too. The Kings, one of San Antonio's largest gangs, recently started accepting young women. Where male gang members used to refer to the girls as "hos and bitches," says Sgt. Kyle Coleman of the Bexar County Sheriff's Department Gang Unit, they're a little more reluctant now as those female gang members start to equal them in fights and drive-by shootings. Girls join gangs for a variety of reasons: protection, fun, because they like a particular boy or

for acceptance. The gangs also provide a makeshift family. Some teens will do anything to join. In one initiation rite in San Antonio, girls are kicked and beaten by half a dozen gang members. In Boston, the two biggest female gangs are every bit as ruthless as the boys'. "They're shooting, stabbing, and they're into drug sales and stickups," says Tracy Litthcut, manager for the Boston Streetworkers violence-intervention program. In New York City, not only are packs of boys "whirlpooling," or surrounding girls in public swimming pools and molesting them, but groups of girls are attacking other female swimmers as well. "I've been amazed at the brutality of the beatings of girls by other girls," says Dr. Naftali Berrill, director of the New York Forensic Mental Health Group. The violence is a vicious, antisocial pack mentality aimed at a target who is incapable of fighting back, says Berrill. The pack smells weakness, and the situation turns into a free-for-all where no individual person feels responsible.

For Further Reflection

Use the following exercises and questions to reflect on the key points in this article.

Who Is a Typical Gang Member?
■ Do you think there is such a thing as a typical gang member? Explain your response.

■ What characteristics seem to be consistent among gang members?

■ What, do you think, are some of the values that support membership in a violent gang?

■ How are those values like or unlike your own values?

■ Jacob distinguishes four groups or types of youth on the street. What are the distinctions? Do those distinctions really make any difference? Why?

Examine the "Ups and Downs" of Gang Membership
■ What good reasons would a gang member give for belonging?

■ Do those reasons seem good to you? Why or why not?

■ What are the dangers of belonging?

■ How do the risks and benefits balance out?

Identify the Risk Factors That Can Lead to Gang Membership

Belonging to a violent gang is often preceded by a cluster of risk factors that make gang membership seem attractive or necessary.

☞ Brainstorm and record a list of those risk factors.

■ How would you describe the role models of at least some gang members?

■ At what age, do you think, do risk factors begin? When do those factors intensify? Why?

■ What can you do to help eliminate or reduce some of those risk factors?

Discuss the Role of the Church in Addressing Gang Activity

One role the church plays is prevention—addressing issues before they deteriorate into crises, as well as building up the body of the faithful. As a church, we probably do better at the latter than the former.

■ Jacob says the church, in his experience, plays a minimal role at best in addressing violent gang behavior. For what reasons might this be true?

■ What programs, curriculum, or support activities does your church have in place to nurture children and teens?

■ What programs, curriculum, or support activities does your church have in place to address the risk factors that could affect any teen?

■ What programs, curriculum, or support activities does your church have in place or in preparation to address the crises of teen violence?

■ How can you help?

Speculate on the Future of a Teen Gang Member

Jacob is right about "ain't looking at 25." An enormous proportion of teens on the street (gang members or not) die before reaching early adulthood.

☞ Distribute paper and markers. Ask each teen to imagine him or herself as a street youth and to depict what life would be like now, in three years, and in five years. The depiction can be in the form of pictures, headlines, words, images, or other symbols.

☞ Ask them to consider how they would eat, where they would find shelter, how they would deal with personal hygiene needs (like having tampons when necessary or where they would go to the bathroom or bathe), how they would deal with their clothing, and what source of income they could anticipate.

☞ Debrief by asking for volunteers to talk about their depictions. Sort out feelings, myths, fears, and facts.

Look at "Soft" Gangs

Not all gangs are murderous street youth. But cliques at school that hang out for self-protection from bullies can use violence, or at least retaliation, as a response to their own victimization.

■ What groups hang out together in your school or community?

■ Would you describe any of them as gangs? Why or why not?

■ What distinguishes those groups from a true gang?

■ What are the boundaries (explicit or implicit) that divide a "bad" gang from a "good" one?

■ What would it take to cross the boundaries? How easy would it be? What factors encourage or discourage crossing over?

Jacob Smith is a 23-year-old former street youth. When he's not out in the field promoting Outward Bound he is spending time with his family, and friends, or dabbling in abstract art (he likes to work with watercolor and oils). He also plays drums, piano, and guitar. Jacob says he "still ain't looking at 25."

Gail Bock is an assistant editor with the Youth Publications Department of The United Methodist Publishing House. She also works on YouthNet and TREK for Jr. High/Middle School.

Surviving Incest

by Sandy Regan

The "Prison"

Sadly, my wonderful escape failed me today. I am locked in my cell once again, and I cannot find my little way out that was so clear and bright to me before. Stiff inside the frozen sheets of my sagging coffin, I force my eyes closed. The prison—not so friendly as I had once thought. It had turned on me and the people inside and made them huge, ugly monsters with sharp objects of torture, nasty yellow claws, drooling teeth, and tongues.

"Oh get me out of here!" shouted the voice in my head. "I . . ." The crash of the cell block door pounds me as I stuff my body deeper into my own cruel resting place. At the sight of my father, I am transfixed in panic-stricken horror as his huge belly, heaving under mad laughter, pours upon me as a welting slime, sizzling the flesh in his own monstrous pan of evil and destruction.

Invasion

"Come here, my child!" he commands, and I collapse onto the floor. I smash my face, my skull into the filthy cement, so cold against my wetting cheek. A massive pain in my brain pulses around the room.

"Hee! Hee! Hee! What fun!" he cackles as the clothes are scattered, as I am shattered across the floor. I am slammed into the cracks, every which way, and from outside myself I turn to watch the devouring of the mindless little body—so motionless, so lifeless, so empty.

"Aaaugh!" groans the monster deep in his satisfaction. "Now let me alone, you bad little girl! How dare you treat your father this way! If your mother were to find out, she would surely leave you for the dogs!"

Dashing for the iron door half dressed, he was wise and sure to leave no traces. The body—my frail and abused body—he twisted back again inside her lace of stain. To me he shouts, "Go down!" quarreling with fumbling limbs and fingers and neck all getting in the way.

Numb from the beating and the body black, red, yellow, purple, and blue—the death was complete and the monster was gone—I had guessed, anyway. The pain was all the same—surely consistent whether he was around or not.

Aftermath

But only ten years later stepping out of my coffin, slowly crawling together again, did I realize my losses, my deep sadness. Held in my hands was my very heart—a gray, shriveling mass—and I began to weep. It was the loss of a father, a childhood. It was not fair. And where was this God the people had been speaking of? How could God let such a horrible thing happen? Had I been forgotten? Damn him!

Visions of my father's death filled me as my eyes bore *hate, hate, hate*. Bitterness engulfed the day to black, and I wore a mission of murder. And so, I build a special cell for father—a lovely coffin with screeching little animals running about—gnawing off toes and ears.

"Hee! Hee! Hee!" whispers the little girl to her father, as satisfaction comes to her. She smiles and closes the cell behind her. "It is your turn."

Searching

And so did the little war continue. "Hack, hack, hack" at Father with the axe in my pocket. Hack until I could hack no more, until I could no longer lift the axe with my bare, bloody fingers.

"I do not understand! Father, how could you do such a thing? I was a little girl; your only daughter! What the hell is the matter with you?"

I kneel to the ground, put my hands together one last time. I *would* see; I would find out now! "God, where are you? Come here, now!"

I wait, watch the sky for some great—I don't know—something. I figure some old guy with a long white beard will fall out of the clouds, and cough and spit all over the place, and say "Whatta ya want, you little whore? I got other people 'sides you."

I wait some more . . . nothing. I sigh, "I knew it; I knew there were no such thing." There never was a voice or movement of the earth that day. Not for a while was God revealed to me.

Healing

So long—I worked many a grueling hour. There came the pain, the rage, the guilt, the pain again. (A vicious cycle, my therapist calls it.) Many times the struggle seemed almost not worth it, and I even came to ask myself—"Wouldn't it be easier just to sink to the bottom of the river and never have to face this cruel world again?" Sad how beautiful this concept became to someone who is so glad to be alive today.

And so there I was, committing to therapy every week, reading every book on the subject I could find, writing and writing in the journal until the morning hours. Healing became almost a passion, a need, a calling. It was my life purpose, you see. If I didn't do this now I would be dead for the rest of my life—buried beneath my own capsule of fear and wounded images; never to breathe a full breath, never to sing the song of revelation. It was the destiny of my soul.

After all, was I going to allow this one man to control me, hurt me, and lock me up for the rest of my life? It was my time to drag myself up off my face and get myself out of that prison. I would do it now, finally. I would be free, finally.

I continued to question myself. "Could I make it? Was I just too stupid, too incapable, too scared?" I didn't know. I guess I took a chance. Anything was better than the prison!

"Goodbye, Father" I whisper, sliding through the cell door. "Hmmmm . . ., strange not to be so trapped." I take a deep breath to hold me to the ground lest I fly away now, a fresh song glorifying my lips.

"Hello world. Hello people. . . . Hello God." I saw God today, arms spread wide for me! Go figure. Perhaps I *would* make it through and I would be all right. What a wonderful thing that will be! Wish me love, okay? See you at the top of the mountain.

For Further Reflection

Sandy uses highly figurative and harsh language to describe her abuse at the hands of her father. Review the segments of her story (summarized below) and talk about the questions. Be sure also to discuss feelings, how to recognize these signs in someone else, and how to make meaning from painful experiences. *If the discussion brings up similar experiences of a group member, be careful with how you proceed. See the section "When Someone Comes to You."*

The *"Prison"* describes Sandy trying to forget or ignore what is happening to her ("I am locked in my cell") by hiding under the covers ("sheets of my coffin") and hoping that no one would hurt her. "The people inside" are those who hurt her, either by direct abuse or through their collusion by silence.

Invasion describes her sexual and physical abuse and the method Sandy's father used to reject and control her afterward.

Aftermath reveals Sandy's pain, and feelings of abandonment or lack of importance to God, and her fantasies of getting even with her father.

Searching continues the theme of looking for God while trying to understand what her father had done to her and why.

Healing describes the long and difficult process of recognizing her pain and letting go, finding out the grace and true nature of God.

■ How did Sandy cope with these horrible experiences?

■ How did Sandy's father keep her from telling anyone what was happening?

■ The abuse stopped when Sandy's parents divorced. Then she could concentrate on understanding rather than survival. How does Sandy describe the aftermath? What are her losses?

■ What was Sandy's original concept of God? What is her later concept? How are they different? How do you think Sandy formed her ideas?

■ What do you see as the elements of Sandy's healing process? How did her opinion of herself change?

Sandy Regan (not her real name) is a seventeen-year-old who loves white-water rafting and soccer. Sandy writes, "What a wonderful day it is when I can share such a story with you and also mention that I have escaped from such a cell. I have traveled along the healing path, and my heart is alive and well and singing because of it. Thank you."

Family Violence

by Donald A. Baker and Mary Eichling

August and his family moved to this country when he was seven and his brother, Ozzie, was one. A year later, their mother died while she was giving birth to James. August's grandmother flew in to help take care of the boys, and she held the family together with her strong hand and will until she died six years later. The following year, August's father, Robert, married Carolyn, who was fifteen years younger than he and only ten years older than August. The following year she give birth to a daughter, Roberta.

During their first eight years in this country, tragedy and turmoil took a toil on August's father, who both resented and depended on August's grandmother's dominant personality. He could never quite grasp the brass ring that this environment held just out of his reach. He resented the "American way of life," which he neither approved of nor fully understood. During recurring periods of unemployment, he became distant and depressed and drank too much. When he drank, he became surly and disciplined his sons with threats of violence. His marriage to Carolyn, though, brought new hope to Robert.

Eight years in America had a very different effect on August. He grew from a wide-eyed seven-year-old into a self-reliant fifteen-year-old. He was convinced that neither his grandmother nor his father really understood the world he was growing up in as well as he did. With his friends at school and in the street he was very open and outgoing. With his family at home he was very quiet and distant.

August was well aware of his father's frustrations, and he sensed his father's self-doubts. After his grandmother died, August became very protective of his younger brothers. He felt he had to teach them about life and protect them from its dangers. When his father's new wife tried to act as their mother, he resented and resisted her. As Carolyn's role in the family grew—and August's defiance grew—Robert's angry threats accelerated.

One night shortly after August's seventeenth birthday, violence erupted. It happened in a flash. Roberta was crying; Carolyn loudly accused James of playing too roughly and told him to go to his room. August told James to stay put and accused Carolyn of playing favorites with her daughter. Robert swatted James while telling him to obey his mother. When August stood up to protect James, Robert pushed him back down on to the couch and told him to treat "me and your mother" with

more respect. August shouted, "She's not my mother, and you don't deserve my respect." When Robert stepped towards him with his hand raised, August picked up a heavy glass ashtray and hit his father. The fight lasted until the police arrived. Fortunately, no one was seriously injured.

What Is Family Violence?

Violence has become one of the most widespread, pervasive threats to families today. The term "domestic violence," until the late 1970's, was used to describe urban riots. Now it is more commonly used when describing family turmoil related to violence within the home, as well as in the surrounding environment.

Environmental violence surrounds families today. The environment of every home offers a unique context of violence that ranges from watching filmed reports of violence on television news and discussing them around the dinner table to living in an housing project where family members must "hit the floor" to dodge bullets flying through windows.

Many families are forced to cope both with social violence, such as poverty and inadequate housing, and with institutions like Aid to Families with Dependent Children (AFDC) and overcrowded housing projects that can provide more anti-family pressure as a by-product of their efforts to respond to the social ills.

Anti-family pressures can just as easily hit the professional, well-to-do family in which the wage earner(s) cope with sixty or more hour work weeks and a deadening travel schedule that dominates their time and attention or the minimum wage laborer whose stress is compounded by long work hours, lack of status, and deadening repetition.

There are many types of stress on the family and its members. Parents who are devalued outside of the family system are more likely to be abusive in the home. Sexual inequality in the work place forces a number of women to remain in violent marriages due to economic pressures.

Home-based violence is always, to some degree, a response to the environmental violence within which every family exists and, to some degree, an individual response.

Families are no longer neatly packaged. A high percentage of families in the 1990's look very different from the 1950's and 60's stereotypes of Ozzie and Harriet and the Cleavers. Rather than a working father and stay-at-home mother with two school-aged children and grandparents living in town, the majority of American families now are a variation on the theme: single parents, remarried parents with stepchildren, adopted children, multiple generations in the same apartment, or extended family living away from grandparents. Each family configuration produces a different set of stresses, many of which we have not yet learned to handle.

Signs of Family Violence

Violence within a family can be so prevalent that it is apparent to all, but it can also be hidden. One of the myths about families is that the shape of the family (two parent, single parent, multi-generational, and so forth) determines whether it functions successfully. In fact, families of all shapes can function wonderfully and families of all shapes can nurture the cycle of violence. Consider the following clues of family violence:

▶ *The family's relationships to friends, relatives, and neighbors.* Be sure to notice the frequency of contact and length of relationship. Is the family isolated or withdrawn? Are they a closed system? Do they seem to have a secret?

▶ *Signs of frustration or failure.* Violence is often a product of unrest, of a perceived impotence, or of a devaluation so comprehensive that only striking out can restore a sense of mastery or even of self.

▶ *Substance abuse.* Look for abuse of alcohol or other drugs.

▶ *Suspicious injuries.* Question frequent bruises or other repeated injuries that are explained away by "accidents."

▶ *Subdued behavior.* Especially among babies and small children, be alerted by listless, withdrawn, frightened, or depressive behavior.

These are only indications of potential problems and are by no means certain proof that family violence is present. Even so, evidence of the listed behaviors, especially in combination with each other, should be seen as red flags.

If The Walls Could Talk

He greets her with a smile as he sits down in his chair,
Reaches with a tender hand to brush aside her hair.
He doesn't seem to give a second
    thought to what he did last night,
And doesn't see she wanted her hair to hide her from his sight.
Is his hand open or closed, or will he choose to bruise with words?
She's always wondering when he says
    he's sorry why does she think it's her.
Too often she knows a side no one else
    has seen,
That the same hand that he uses in love
    he uses to give her pain.

If the walls could talk, they'd tell of your pain.
How you dream it will change and not be so insane.
You have been broken by the one who loves you so.
If the walls could talk they would tell you to go.

Hmmm, just a little boy sitting on a swing.
Feet don't even touch the ground. He doesn't say a thing.
He had heard the angry words screamed last night again.
Was he to blame 'cause he heard his name so he just covered
  his head.
These should be the happiest days of a life that just began,
But his eyes show fear beyond his years and his heart began to
  harden.
Children raising children, the only difference is years.
He asked for little, got only less. Now only the walls hear.

If the walls could talk, they'd tell of your pain.
How you dream it will change and not be so insane.
You have been broken by the ones who love you so.
If the walls could talk they would tell you to go.

Consequences of Family Violence

Many studies have shown that the majority of abusive adults were themselves abused as children. As in the lyrics to the song "If The Walls Could Talk" imply, children internalize violence and, frequently, carry it with them into adulthood.

The primary responsibility of a family is to provide a nurturing, safe environment that encourages growth and development. Issues of authority and control become paramount as family members struggle to develop and change roles. Confusion with these issues can lead to a devaluation of individual members that breeds an atmosphere lacking intimacy and affection.

Whatever the shape of the family and the character of the stress they experience, home-based family violence devastates every family member. Violent acts may occur within different family contexts and settings with varying degrees of motivation or they may stem from different relationships, but in all cases, how we express our anger toward family members imprints a lasting impression on children.

Children raised in violent homes have much the same reaction as children who have experienced the trauma of war. To a child, family violence is a personal endorsement of violence from someone who is loved, trusted, respected, and depended upon. To both a child and a teen, this endorsement of violence, be it verbal or physical, carries primary authority and the weight of the world.

What Can a Teen in a Violent Family Do?

Teens who live in violent families need to know that violence at home is not usual, not normal, not acceptable, and does not have to be endured.

Teens who live in violent families need to know that help is available. Change and healing within a violent family begins by breaking vows of secrecy, by dropping out of the conspiracy of silence. It's important that teens in this situation tell a pastor, Sunday school teacher, school teacher, counselor, social worker, coach, police officer, relative, neighbor, friend, parent, or someone else they can trust. It's important that they tell a responsible, sympathetic adult. It is important that they GET HELP!

Teens who live in violent families need to know that they are loved. They are loved by God and they are loved by God's people.

What Can God's People Do?

Children and teens need protection from violence within families until intervention and treatment can be accomplished.

Teenagers who learn of a friend living in a violent family can help by encouraging their friend to seek help. They can help that friend figure out who to go to. They can offer to go with that friend. If they are afraid to seek help themselves, they can offer to go for help for that friend.

If a teen is not sure about what is happening in a friend's family, or if that friend declines help, encourage that teen to tell what they know to a responsible, sympathetic adult. Describing what is seen to someone who is knowledgeable, trained, and experienced will help sort things out.

Responsible adults who learn of a child or teen living in a violent home have both a moral and a legal responsibility to report their knowledge to legal authorities—the police, the state child welfare agency, or both. (See the article, "Legal Knowledge Is Key" beginning on page 12.)

Healing can come to violent families first through external controls, and then through family members learning new ways of dealing with each other. Families can confront and change their patterns of violence with exciting successes. Family violence is changeable through interventions that provide support to and encourage healing for all family members.

Churches can minister to families struggling with violence and protect victimized family members by:

▶ Reaching out to marginal members of the community and inviting them into the church's fellowship.

▶ Recognizing that violence can disrupt families of every description.

▶ Training pastors, Sunday school teachers, youth group leaders, youth choir directors, and all workers to look for and to see the signs of family violence and to respond when those signs appear.

▶ Advocating for systems that support families rather than add to their stress.

▶ Witnessing to God's loving and healing presence in the world.

For Further Reflection

Use the example of August's story as well as your own experience to reflect on issues surrounding family violence.

Look at the Family
■ What is a family?

■ August's family took four different shapes during the course of ten years. Can you list them? (*Two parents with children, father and grandmother with children, single father with children, second marriage with a child and half-brothers*)

■ What were the different stresses August's family experienced as its shape changed?

■ What are the shapes of the families of the members of your group? What other shapes can families take?

■ What are the stresses that families of other shapes can experience?

Investigate the Family Environment
■ What is a "family environment"?

■ August's family had to deal with being new in this country and with being poor. How did those external factors add to a climate of violence for them?

■ What other family environments have the potential to nurture violent situations? How?

Study the Forms of Family Violence
■ What forms can family violence take?

■ What form did violence in August's family take?

■ What form did family violence take for the children in the song "If The Walls Could Talk"?

■ What other examples of internal, home-based family violence can you identify? What are the signs?

Consider Who Is Responsible for Family Violence
■ Who is responsible for family violence? Give reasons for your answer.

■ Who was responsible for the violence in August's family? Was any one person responsible? Why?

■ Give an example of a situation where one person clearly is responsible for the violence within a family. What makes this situation different than that of August's family? Give reasons for your answer.

Review the Indicators of Family Violence
■ What are indicators of family violence?

■ Who within August's family has authority or control during each stage of the story? How can you tell?

■ What are some of the indicators of violence in August's family that might have been visible to others outside the family?

■ What role do you think alcohol played in the violence in August's family?

■ What other indicators might one look for in other families?

Anticipate the Consequences of Family Violence
■ What are the consequences of family violence?

■ What assumptions about himself did the boy in "If The Walls Could talk" make? What assumptions about violence does he make? How can you tell?

■ How did his assumptions affect his behavior when he became an adult? Did it have to be that way? Give reasons for your response.

■ How can we intervene and support a family that is experiencing violence?

■ How might you have helped August's family if you had known them?

■ The police were alerted to the situation within August's family. If they had not been, should some one have notified the authorities? Why or why not?

■ Who could have helped the boy in "If The Walls Could Talk"? As a young boy, he suffered in silence. How might someone have found out about his hurt?

Strategies for How You and Your Church Can Help
■ How could the church have helped August or the children in the song? What can you do?

■ What can your church do to identify families that are experiencing violence in your town?

■ What can your church do to be prepared to help a family that is experiencing violence, in your town?

■ What can your church do to help prevent violence in your town?

Reverend Don Baker started reaching out to at-risk youth in Evanston, Illinois as a student intern at Garrett Theological Seminary twenty-six years ago. He has been the Executive Director of Youth Organizations Umbrella, Inc. in Evanston since 1972. Don, his wife Patty, their son Andy, and their daughter Abby live in Evanston.

Mary T. Eichling has a Master's in Counseling from the University of Virginia. She has worked in the child welfare field for twenty years. She has co-authored curriculum for Foster Parent Training and has led numerous workshops.

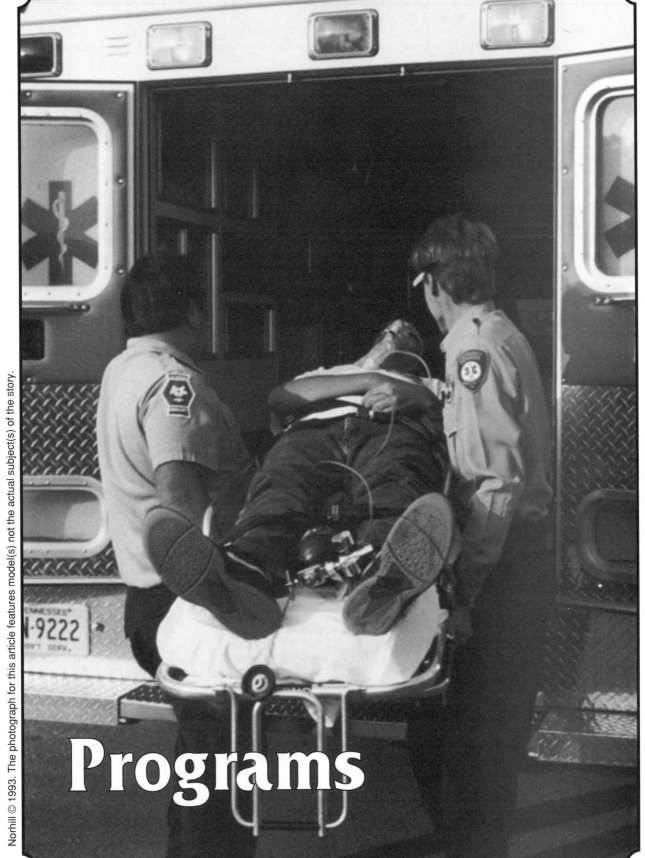

Programs

Discipline or Abuse?

by Keith Drew

PURPOSE: To help youth recognize the differences between discipline and abuse and to help them identify what to do when the lines between them are blurred.

Preparation

Before using this program, consult with area school counselors or local church pastors to determine what specific resources are available in the community. (Possible resources are listed starting on page 90.) Consider inviting one or more helping professional to be a part of the group's discussion. (See the section "When Someone Comes to You.")

Be prepared, also, for the possibility that someone in the youth group is a victim of abuse. Emotional scars as a result of family abuse and violence are often hidden and difficult to recognize. However, depending on your group members and their openness to sharing with one another, someone may reveal a painful personal experience of this sort. Schedule enough time during the session for an adequate response to any such conversation that may occur.

Ideally, parents should also be involved with this topic. A separate meeting for parents, held at the same time, might provide the beginning point for a useful dialogue among youth group members, their parents, and others in the congregation or community.

Also, for this session you will need:
♦ large pieces of paper and markers
♦ pencils or pens and paper
♦ Bibles and relevant commentaries
♦ song books or hymnals and printed statements for worship
♦ preprinted statements for worship

Discipline: Definitions and Responsibility

Appropriate discipline is the means by which a parent teaches or trains a child to develop self-control, character, or orderliness and efficiency. From a Christian perspective, discipline is positive teaching, exercised in godly love, that encourages a person's growth. Discipline often involves the setting and enforcing of rules. Parents also need to function as a positive role model for their children. Both children and parents have guidelines and responsibilities for discipline within the home.

☞ Write the following definitions on a large piece of paper. Ask the group members first to paraphrase the meanings and then to discuss them.

■ DISCIPLINE—a process of learning or training that develops self-control, character, or orderliness and efficiency.

■ DISCIPLE—a learner or follower, literally, one who learns.

A Biblical Basis

Our image of God as Father, or a loving parent, stems from appropriate models for discipline offered by the Bible.

☞ Form five teams, and assign one of these Scripture references to each team.
Exodus 34:6-7 God is merciful
Proverbs 13:24 Spare the rod?
Matthew 7:9-11 How much more God gives
Ephesians 6:1-4 Advice for families
2 Timothy 4:1-2 Convince, rebuke, encourage

☞ Ask each team to consider the following questions, and then bring all the group members together for a discussion of their responses.

■ What does the passage say about discipline and punishment?

■ Does God ever discipline us? punish us? Why? How?

■ What, do you think, does the passage mean now for parents and their children?

Recognizing Abusive Situations

Sometimes the stresses and strains of life impair one's judgment and lead to irrational and destructive behavior. As imperfect humans, some parents forget (or maybe never learned) the boundaries separating discipline and abuse. Most parents or relatives don't start out with the intention of abusing the ones they love. Often, abuse is a link in a long chain of events, beginning when the abuser himself or herself suffered abuse. While childhood trauma does not justify violent or harmful actions, such a background gives a clue as to what shapes some persons' behavior.

One thing must be made clear: *Children (no matter what age) are not responsible for the behavior of abusive parents.* This is one of the most difficult facts for children and teens in abusive situations to understand. Though they are not to blame for parental abuse and neglect, they often feel and/or have been told that they are.

☞ Post these three signs at different places in the room: "Proper Discipline," "Not Sure," and "A Form of Abuse."

☞ Ask the group members to review the sidebar information in "Signs of Abuse." Then read aloud the following cases one by one. Ask them to stand near the posted sign that indicates their opinion of the behaviors described in each case.

☞ Engage the participants in a discussion of their responses and their reasons for those responses. Ask persons who stand at "A Form of Abuse" to indicate what kind of abuse they think it is and why.

Bill's dad asked Bill to clean out the garage right away. However, Bill goofed around and did not start on the chore immediately. When his dad stepped into the garage and saw that Bill had just begun the task, he angrily grabbed a thin slat of wood and smacked Bill once hard on the thigh.

Jenny's uncle had come to visit. She didn't realize he was in the hall right outside the bathroom when she finished taking her shower. As she stepped into the hallway, Uncle Ed tugged at the lapel of Jenny's bathrobe and said, "Let's see what a beautiful young lady you have become."

Victor's mother is easily irritated and when annoyed by something that involves Victor, frequently mutters comments such as, "Why would anyone want to have children?" She never says this directly to Victor but she makes sure he can hear it.

Hae Sun's older sister was furious because Hae Sun had accidentally embarrassed her. She threatened to do something really drastic because of the shame Hae Sun had caused her. She locked herself in her room for three hours and wouldn't open the door or speak to Hae Sun. When she finally came out, she said, "Gee, I was just kidding."

Tom's foster family is adjusting to having a new member who is new to their way of doing things and to the rules of their household. Everyone in the family is explaining, at length and often, "how things work in *this* family."

☞ Have the group members discuss how they might talk to a parent or other relative when experiencing abuse. Be sure to emphasize that there are *always* options for a victim of abuse. Some of the circumstances and/or influences that might lead a parent to be abusive with his or her child are mentioned in the sidebar "Factors Behind Abuse" on page 56.

SIGNS OF ABUSE

▶ **Physical Abuse**—face slappings; beatings or lashings; kicking any part of the anatomy; gagging of the mouth; binding with ropes or other materials; severe spankings; breaking bones; burns inflicted with scalding water, cigarette butts, and so forth; withholding food for a prolonged length of time

▶ **Sexual Abuse**—any unwelcome intimate physical contact, especially involving the genitals; forced intimate contact that usually occurs outside accepted avenues for sexual expression; may involve a parent or another relative and a child or any adult and child or young person

▶ **Psychological Abuse**—may accompany any of the other types of abuse; any form of abuse in which negative coercion is used to inhibit the natural, healthy growth of one's self-image; mind games

▶ **Emotional Abuse**—closely related to psychological abuse; can include the persistent degrading of an individual's feelings of self-worth; verbal battering that involves the use of such terms as "stupid" and "worthless;" can include the withholding of touch or communication

▶ **Verbal Abuse**—a form of psychological abuse, verbal abuse can accompany either physical, emotional, or sexual abuse; an attempt to dominate someone through aggressive verbal statements

FACTORS BEHIND ABUSE

▶ Alcoholism

▶ Use of other drugs (even some forms of prescription drugs)

▶ Money problems

▶ Job-related stresses

▶ Spiritual immaturity

▶ Emotional and social immaturity (getting married/having children too early)

▶ Poor role models for parenthood

▶ Abuse suffered as a child

▶ Inability to express emotions in a healthful manner

▶ Inability to express needs to spouse in a healthful manner

▶ Strained relationship with spouse

▶ Prolonged or severe physical illness

▶ Any form of mental illness

▶ Inability to cope with the demands of parenting

What To Do When You Suspect Abuse

Some youth may find it helpful to practice coping with and confronting a fictional example of abuse or discipline.

☞ Review the coping strategies mentioned below.

☞ Ask for several volunteers to choose one of the cases used earlier and to develop a roleplay that acts out one or more of the coping strategies. Refer to the sidebar "Factors Behind Abuse" for other ideas.

☞ Be sure all group members have a chance to debrief.

1. *Analyze the behavior.* Is this an isolated incident, a pattern, or the beginning of a pattern of abuse or violence? Are this person's actions abnormal? A spanking, especially of a small child, is not necessarily abuse. However, any discipline that turns into punishment accompanied by violence, rage, or neglect must be looked at carefully.

2. *Validate the behavior.* (Validate does not mean condone.) Instead, check out the specific behavior with a friend or a trusted adult. Is the behavior, in fact, excessive or violent? Has a father or a mother, for example, overstepped accepted limits for showing affection toward his or her daughter or son?

3. *Confront the persons involved.* Often, those who are being violated or abused are experiencing denial. If you believe someone you know or love is being abused, try to speak to her or him about the problem in a calm and rational manner. If you are the one being violated, you may be able to talk with the parent or family member who is harming you.

4. *Seek help.* Abuse is a complex issue, and teens may not be able to (and should not have to) confront a situation alone. While peer support may be tremendously valuable emotionally, it still may not provide necessary protection for the person who is being abused. Seek the aid of a trusted adult or of others in a similar situation for support and training to learn the best response to instances of abuse.

---

1. *Analyze behavior*
2. *Validate behavior*
3. *Confront persons involved*
4. *Seek help*

Going the Second Mile

If the group members want to do further research on the subject of abuse, the local library is a good place to start. The following title is among potential resources to investigate: *Coping With Family Violence,* revised edition by Morton L. Kurland (Rosen Group, 1990).

Find out what support groups for teens are available in your area. If none exist, discuss with other youth leaders the possibility of forming such a group at a local church or school.

Worship

Sing either "We Are One in the Spirit" or "There Is a Balm in Gilead," (*The United Methodist Hymnal* No. 375).

Say "Peace be with you" as you offer signs of peace to one another (by shaking hands, hugging, and so forth).

Prepare each of the following statements ahead of time on separate pieces of paper. Have the group members sit in a circle. Ask several of the youth to read the statements aloud, followed by a moment for silent reflection.

* Please, Mom and Dad, really listen to what I have to say.

* Please, Mom and Dad, don't nag me every minute of the day and don't make me feel dumb when I make mistakes.

* Please, Mom and Dad, don't expect perfection in everything I do; just love me for trying.

* Please, Mom and Dad, remember that I am neither a child nor an adult; sometimes I don't understand and I need understanding.

* Please, Mom and Dad, love and accept me for who I am, not just for the things I can do.

Pray this prayer together: "O, God, help us and our family members to grow closer to you and to one another, as we learn to accept and love one another just as you have created us. In Jesus' name. Amen."

© 1992 by Cokesbury

Keith Drew is a pastor in the North Georgia Annual Conference. Keith has a specialized degree in ministry to the youth culture from Iliff School of Theology and has years of experience working with youth and parents.

Find out what support groups for teens are available in your area. If none exist, discuss with other youth leaders the possibility of forming such a group at a local church or school.

You're Too Close

by Charles Lewis

PURPOSE: To help youth deal with unwelcome sexual or physical advances.

Preparation

Invite to this meeting a counselor who knows the resources available for youth who have been sexually abused. Invite your pastor only if he or she has been trained as a counselor and feels comfortable talking about sexual abuse. The counselor you choose should be someone to whom the youth relate well. He or she should be available during the entire program as well as for the last activity, "Where Can I Get Help?" If possible, involve the counselor in planning the program.

In addition, gather Bibles, commentaries, and volunteers for the skit.

Eric's Day in Court

The following skit will dramatize some of the problems and issues that a youth must ultimately address if he or she has been subjected to unwanted sexual advances by an adult or other teen. Though this setting is a courtroom, not all confrontations are handled through the legal system.

☞ Invite four youth to present a skit. The person playing the part of Eric must be male; the other three characters can be male or female (you may have to change their names).

☞ Ask the actors to rehearse the skit several times. They do not need to memorize their lines, but they should be able to read without stumbling and with appropriate emotion.

(The skit is part of a divorce and custody hearing. Eric Andrews is sitting in the witness stand. Judge Roger Nelson is behind the bench. Prosecuting attorney Diane Czaja is asking questions. Psychologist Linda Walker is sitting nearby. As the scene opens, Eric is obviously distressed.)

DIANE: Eric, please tell the court what happened before your parents separated.

ERIC (*blinking and swallowing hard between sentences*): I was getting undressed to take a shower. Suddenly I realized my mother had opened the door and was watching me. I grabbed a towel and asked her to leave. Instead, she walked over and pulled the towel away. "I just want a hug, honey," she said. "You aren't going to try to make it something dirty, are you?"

DIANE: What happened then?

ERIC: I didn't want to make a scene. I mean, she is my mother, so I let her hug me. But she started rubbing her hands over me and kissing me. Then she began to fondle me. I pushed her away and must have yelled at her, because the next thing I knew, Dad was standing there. He made my mother get away from me. A few days later, we moved into an apartment and Dad filed for divorce.

DIANE: Was this the first time she had approached you sexually?

ERIC (*hesitating and stumbling over his words*): Uh, well, I mean, she was always affectionate, but nothing. . .

JUDGE: Eric, remember you are under oath. You must tell us the truth.

ERIC (*placing his head in his hands*): No. It began nine years ago when Dad started working the night shift at the hospital. I was pretty little then, and sometimes I got scared at night. Mom had me sleep with her so I wouldn't be frightened. But then she wanted me to sleep naked so I wouldn't get too warm. After that she began fondling me. Finally, about three years ago, she made me have sex with her. At first, I didn't realize what was going on. Later, I asked her to stop, but she told me that if I said anything, Dad wouldn't love me any more and that they would get a divorce. I didn't think anyone would believe me. And here we are, anyway. I feel so ashamed.

DIANE: Thank you, Eric. You may be seated now. (*She turns to the judge.*) Your Honor, I would like to call to the stand Dr. Linda Walker, a well-known psychologist. (*Dr. Walker is placed under oath.*)

DIANE: Dr. Walker, what is your experience with victims of abuse?

LINDA: People who report being sexually abused almost never lie about what happened. Sexual abuse is more common than you might think.

DIANE: Who abuses them?

LINDA: In many cases, a parent. But older brothers and sisters, uncles and aunts, or family friends are often involved. Unfortunately, the victims usually don't report the abuse. They worry about what will happen to the offender, or they feel they are somehow responsible for what happened.

DIANE: Are they responsible?

LINDA: Absolutely not. The victims are never to blame. Even if the sexual encounter is not forced upon them physically, the abuser often plays on their fears. And they still feel shame, as Eric does. So, in addition to stopping the abusers, it's important for victims to get counseling.

☞ Ask for reactions to the skit—feelings, impressions, questions.

JUST THE FACTS

Extent of Sexual Abuse

▶ Childhood sexual abuse reports account for approximately 12 percent of all reported child abuse in the United States—almost 360,000 cases per year.

▶ About 19 percent of the female and 9 percent of the male college students studied say they were sexually victimized as children.

▶ Half of all sexual abuse of children occurs within the family.

▶ At least 1 million children are physically abused by their parents or caretakers every year.

▶ About 2,000 children die of physical abuse and neglect each year.

Characteristics of Sexual Abuse

Sexual abuse usually occurs when a child is between the age of 9 and 12. The abuser is almost always male, usually known to the child, and often a relative. Such abuse is not usually limited to a single episode, and does not usually involve force. All racial, ethnic, and economic groups are represented in these cases.

(Reprinted by permission from *"The Youth Ministry Resource Book,"* copyright 1988, edited by Eugene C. Roehlkepartain. Published by Group Books, Box 481, Loveland, CO 80539, pages 180-181.)

God's Response

This exercise will help group members develop a biblical base for their thinking.

☞ Distribute Bibles and the appropriate commentaries. Form three small groups.

☞ Ask each group to read and study these Scriptures: **1 Corinthians 3:16-17**, **Exodus 20:12**, and **Leviticus 18:6-17**.

☞ Lead the youth in discussing some of the issues related to unwanted advances, using the following questions:

■ The fifth commandment tells us to honor our parents. How should we react if they ask us to do something that makes us feel uncomfortable?

■ Sometimes we aren't sure if someone is playing rough, showing affection, or being abusive. How can we determine what kind of touching is appropriate and what is not?

■ How should a teenager react if he or she is uncomfortable with the way someone touches him or her?

■ Should a teenager who feels that he or she has been physically or sexually molested by a trusted adult, especially a family member, tell someone about his or her experience? If so, who? How much should he or she tell?

■ Reporting an incident involving an adult could cause him or her to be arrested. Should the victim report the incident anyway? Why or why not?

■ What should a teenager do if he or she thinks that reporting sexual or physical abuse would cause his or her parents to divorce? Why?

■ What should a teenager do if the abuser asks him or her to promise not to tell? if a promise has already been made? Give reasons for your responses.

What should a teenager do if he or she tells about his or her experience and no one believes him or her? What if the teenager is accused of causing the incident?

■ Do you think victims of physical or sexual abuse are ever responsible? Why or why not?

How Would You Handle This?

☞ Invite volunteers to roleplay two or three of the following situations. If the youth have done roleplays before, read the situations aloud and encourage them to act spontaneously. Otherwise, give them a few minutes to consider the situation before they perform.

☞ If you wish, discuss the situations as case studies rather than acting them out.

☞ Following each of the roleplays or cases, ask:

■ What happened?

■ What worked well? Why?

■ What might you do differently another time? Why?

■ What other options or solutions can you think of?

■ Ask the group: If you were in a similar situation, how would you respond?

Remind youth that while friends can help each other by talking over their experiences, trusted adults may have the best access to (or power base for) effective help and change.

1. Brenda has been babysitting for Mr. Thompson for six months. Tonight as he is driving her home, he places his hand on her leg. When she objects, he says he is just being friendly. "I have a child of my own, you know," he says. She still objects, and he threatens to tell her parents that she tried to make a pass at him. How should she react?

2. Leonard is visiting a friend when his friend's mother enters the room dressed only in revealing underwear. When Leonard looks startled, she laughs at him. "I'm old enough to be your mother," she says, but makes no effort to get dressed. Leonard's friend doesn't seem to feel comfortable either, but he says nothing. How should Leonard react?

3. Daniel has been active in a boy's group for several years and has grown to like his group leader. Recently he has felt uncomfortable with the way the leader hugs the boys and wraps his arms around their shoulders. Daniel and the group leader are checking out a new camp site when the leader suggests they go skinny dipping in the creek. How should Daniel react?

4. Kathy's brother has always been physically affectionate, but as he has grown older, his touches have been more and more intimate. Today, for the third time this week, he "accidentally" rests his hand on her breast. How should Kathy react?

5. Bev and Jake have been dating for several months and seem very happy together. Jake sits near Lisa in chemistry class and Lisa has made no secret of her attraction to him. Thinking only that it would be friendly, Jake has sat with Lisa a few times at lunch, and hasn't mentioned it to Bev. Lisa is getting verbally obnoxious with Bev and is calling Jake several times every evening. Today Lisa has hovered near Bev at every opportunity and each time has flashed a knife. How should Bev and Jake react?

Where Can I Get Help?

Ask the counselor to talk about where the youth can get help if they feel someone is encroaching or threatening them. In addition to emphasizing the availability of professional counselors, be sure to tell the group that if they need help, they can come to church youth leaders, teachers at school, or other adults. Remind youth that while friends can help each other by talking over their experiences, trusted adults may have the best access to (or power base for) effective help and change. If a teenager tells a friend about experiences of abuse or threat, the friend should encourage the victim to contact an adult; or the friend should report the incident to someone they both trust.

Conclude the program by asking the counselor to address the feelings of guilt victims often experience and especially the guilt they may feel when trapped in a situation they feel powerless to change.

Worship

Ask one person (perhaps the group leader) to sit in front of the group with his or her back to the group. Dim the lights so that, if possible, he or she is silhouetted. Invite the group to sing a hymn or song of trust in God.

Then ask the group to participate in the following litany, reading their responses from **Psalm 23**:

LEADER: I feel so dirty. If people knew what has happened to me, they'd never speak to me.

GROUP: (*Read Psalm 23, verse 1.*)

LEADER: At times, I can't sleep, thinking about what has happened.

GROUP: (*Read verse 2.*)

LEADER: Sometimes, I feel that even God doesn't love me. How can God forgive me for what I've done?

GROUP: (*Read verse 3.*)

LEADER: I tell myself it's not my fault, and in my mind I know it's not, but I still feel guilty. People try to make me feel better, and I know they mean well, but it doesn't seem to help.

GROUP: (*Read verse 4.*)

LEADER: When I think about the person who has done this to me, I get so angry. I know I'm supposed to forgive others, but I can't.

GROUP: (*Read verse 5.*)

LEADER: God, grant me your peace.

GROUP: (*Read verse 6.*)

Conclude the worship service with silent prayer.

© 1991 by Graded Press.

Charles Lewis is an English teacher and a free-lance writer in Fitzgerald, Georgia. When he's not driving his students up the wall, Charles spends free time with his wife, who is also a teacher (English and Latin). They enjoy reading, traveling, walking, and soaking in their hot tub. They have one daughter, who is married, and a cat who spends his time fighting over the easy chair.

No Means No, Doesn't It?

by Patty Reed

PURPOSE: To help youth understand the facts of date/acquaintance rape and think about ways to prevent its occurrence.

The topic of date rape and the attitudes surrounding the occurrence of date/acquaintance rape are the subjects of this two-part program. Part 1, "No Means No, Doesn't It?" deals with basic facts about date/acquaintance rape. Part 2, "If Rape Isn't Sex, What Is It?" looks at attitudes and beliefs about date/acquaintance rape, perceptions about men and women, and information about rape prevention.

Preparation Guidelines

☞ Because the topic of rape and sexual violence is sensitive, give information about the program plans to the pastor and/or other appropriate church leaders. Consider sending a letter about the date/acquaintance rape programs to the youths' parents or guardians.

☞ Some schools offer programs dealing with date/acquaintance rape. Find out what is available to the youth outside of the church. Maintain an open and caring atmosphere during these programs.

☞ Be careful not to probe for personal information the youth seem unwilling to mention. A nonjudgmental attitude on the part of leaders is absolutely critical.

☞ Refer to the section "Where to Go for Help" beginning on page 90 for information on "What to Do in Case of Date/Acquaintance Rape."

☞ If at all possible, plan these sessions with a rape or crisis counselor who can help lead. If you are not able to locate a rape counsellor through the nearest rape and sexual abuse center, the community health office, or the health center of a college or university, make use of the resources listed on pages 92-93 and other resources available in your community libraries or agencies. Be prepared to provide information on where the youth can go for confidential rape counselling.

☞ Copy on a chalkboard or on posterboard the closing prayer to use after this session and the next.

Planning Part 1

If possible, plan your program with the assistance of the rape counsellor. Discuss your intentions for this program, possible responses from the group, time availability, and who is responsible for which parts of the sessions.

☞ Include these topics in the first session:

Why this is a youth issue

▶ Victims of date/acquaintance rape are usually high school or college age youth.

▶ Four out of five (or more) teenage victims of rape are sexually assaulted by someone they know.

▶ Date/acquaintance rape (forced sex without one's consent) is wrong under all circumstances.

What is date/acquaintance rape? or How a date turns into a crime

▶ Two people start off being together for friendly reasons and then something goes wrong. If one person wants to have sex and the other says no, it is NEVER okay to force the other person, regardless of how he or she act.

▶ If one person forces another to submit to sexual intercourse against her or his will, rape has occurred regardless of the couple's relationship. This is true regardless of the sex of the persons.

▶ Rape is an act of domination. Many people think that rape is sex. It is not sex. It is VIOLENCE using sexual acts.

▶ When either the female or the male is unable to think clearly due to the use of alcohol and/or other drugs, an intimate situation can quickly get out of hand.

▶ Rape can happen anywhere. The victim's or offender's home, car, or some other familiar place is often the location of a date/acquaintance rape.

Prevention and protection

▶ If teenagers of both sexes become aware of how date/acquaintance rape happens, they can start to take steps to protect themselves.

Dating Is Good, Usually

Dating *is* good and should be a normal, healthy, and fun way to learn important lessons about making, keeping, and sometimes breaking relationships. The object of this topic is not to scare teens or set up anyone as ogres. Because so few people understand date/acquaintance rape until it is too late, the purpose here is to provide information to keep dating healthy and appropriate.

☞ Introduce the program by reading or paraphrasing the first paragraph in this section. Talk about these remarks and the questions that follow. (The "Findings and Facts" information in the box below will be used later.)

■ How many of you have ever heard of date/acquaintance rape?

■ How many of you think that date/acquaintance rape is okay or something that cannot be prevented in some situations?

■ How much do you know about date/acquaintance rape? Where or how did you learn what you know?

Findings and Facts About Rape

▶ Four out of five teenage rape victims are assaulted by someone they know.

▶ Of these victims, 56 percent are raped on a date.

▶ 30 percent are raped by a friend.

▶ 11 percent are raped by a boyfriend.

▶ 78 percent of rape victims do not tell their parents.

▶ 71 percent of rape victims confide in a friend or friends.

▶ Only 6 percent of date/acquaintance rapes are reported to the police.

▶ Date/acquaintance rape is as traumatic and serious as other types of rape.

▶ Date/acquaintance rape is against the law.

▶ Date/acquaintance rape is not the victim's fault.

▶ Forcing sex on an unwilling partner is never okay.

▶ A person always has the right to (and SHOULD) say no to unwanted sexual activity.

Some Dates Aren't Fun

IMPORTANT NOTE: Statistics unfortunately suggest that you are likely to have in your group even very young teens who have experienced rape or sexual abuse. Be sensitive to this possibility and be prepared to provide appropriate crisis assistance should this come up.

☞ After discussing the introductory questions, form at least two separate age-level groups. Dealing with this particular topic by age level is important because many younger youth have no dating experiences and are just beginning to deal with their sexuality.

For Younger Youth:

☞ Ask the youth if they have ever received an obscene phone call or seen a "flasher." They may feel more comfortable at first discussing the non-touching forms of sexual abuse, which also include voyeurism (peeping Toms) child pornography, and abusive sexual comments.

☞ Have the teens describe their feelings about having to observe or be a party to any of these activities with negative sexual overtones.

☞ Have the participants act out a roleplay that involves dating or some other social occasion. Use one of these situations or make up your own.

1. You are at a school event. You see a couple sneaking off from the gym down a darkened hall. They are laughing and walking close together. It looks like their hands are wandering too.

2. You are at the mall with a bunch of friends. You see the 17-year-old brother of another friend (who is not with you). He offers to give you a ride home. You're not sure, but think he smells a little like beer. He's being VERY friendly.

3. You hear a bunch of guys in the cafeteria talking about one of the girls in your class. Most of their remarks are about her good looks and her nice body, but the guys are using vulgar terms, which are clearly not compliments.

■ How could the situation turn into date/acquaintance rape?

■ What attitudes do you notice? Which ones seem to value persons and which ones devalue? Why?

■ Have you seen an example of date/acquaintance rape in a movie or on television? How did it start? What did the persons do to get in the situation? How did it end? (This may be the only exposure that members of this age group have to date/acquaintance rape.)

For Older Youth:

Someone in this group of teens may have been raped or may have raped someone. In one survey of high school students, more than half the males and perhaps one-third of the females thought forced sex was acceptable if the girl "got the boy excited," or "led him on," or had said yes but then changed her mind. If either victims or victimizers are present, this program will no doubt stir up powerful and painful memories and may change her or his perceptions of what happened. Be ready to deal sensitively with questions and with emotional reactions, including that of rage.

☞ Based on the responses to the introductory questions, the rape counselor (or group leader) should openly and directly discuss the facts in "Findings and Facts About Rape." Use the following questions to facilitate the discussion.

■ Do you think it is ever okay to force someone to have sex? Why, or why not?

■ Many rape victims will talk to a friend but not to a parent. Why, do you think, is this so?

■ Why, do you think, are so few rape cases reported to the authorities?

■ How do you think you would feel about telling someone if you were attacked?

When Dating Is a Crime

☞ Go over the information in "Why This Is a Youth Issue" and "How a Date Turns into a Crime" on page 62. You may want to turn the facts into a questionnaire. (For example: How old is the usual victim of date rape? What percentage of persons are raped by someone they know? Is rape the same thing as sex?)

☞ After conducting the survey, discuss answers and refer again to those two sections to help teens better understand date/acquaintance rape.

☞ You may want to discuss the responses in two age-level groups or in same-sex groups and then talk about the findings with the whole group. Keep the conversation centered on the facts. If you are planning a second program, tell the youth that the next session will deal with attitudes.

How to Cut the Risks

☞ Bring the groups back together. Introduce the concept that if teenagers of both sexes become aware of how date/acquaintance rape happens, and what it is, they can start to take steps to protect themselves. Note that a fuller discussion of prevention will be presented in the next session.

☞ Remember to include a short question-and-answer time. Also make yourself available for additional conversation after the meeting.

> *In one survey of high school students, more than half the males and perhaps one-third of the females thought forced sex was acceptable if the girl "got the boy excited," or "led him on," or had said yes but then changed her mind.*

The Bible's Response

Jesus understood the damaging effects of violence, especially of acts of violence committed against neighbors, friends, or even family. Look at the following two passages and ask the youth to insert date/acquaintance rape somewhere in the passages.

☞ Assign to *younger youth* Matthew 18:1-7.

☞ Assign to *older youth* Matthew 5:21-26.

☞ Discuss the following questions.

■ What do you think Jesus is saying to youth in this passage?

■ How would you put the passage into your own words, using date rape somewhere in it?

■ (For younger youth) What is a stumbling block? If a teen is raped by a friend or on a date, how might that experience turn into a stumbling block?

Worship

Gather in a circle. **Say** to the group members: "Violence has never been and will never be an expression of love; rape, because it is a violent act that is harmful to another person, is always wrong."

Pray together the following prayer:

O God of peace and God of justice, who delivers us from captivity, we know that you observe the violence that appears throughout human history and weep, not only for the victims, but also for the victimizers.

Grant peace to all who suffer the effects of brutality and renew their faith in your protection and care. Help us respect one another's choices.

Thank you, God, for creating us male and female. We affirm the goodness of our sexuality. Help us to see all members of your creation as you do. In Jesus' name. **Amen.**

Close with a hymn or song.

© 1993 by Cokesbury.

Patricia Reed lives in Alexandria, Virginia. She helps coordinate the Gleaning Network in the Washington, DC area and works with the Harvest of Hope program. Patty was a member of the design team for Forum '92 and was elected secretary of FAYM (Forum for Adults in Youth Ministry). As a Navy wife and mother of two teenagers, she has lived in ten cities coast to coast and has enjoyed a wide variety of church experiences. Patty has her own desktop publishing business and gets creative on her Macintosh computer and her weaving loom.

If any of you put a stumbling block before one of these little ones who believe in me, it would be better for you if a great millstone were fastened around your neck and you were drowned in the depth of the sea.

Matthew 18:6

If Rape Isn't Sex, What Is It?

by Patty Reed and Laurel Schneider

PURPOSE: To help youth become aware of cultural perceptions of gender, attitudes, and peer pressures that can encourage date/acquaintance rape, as well as ways to prevent date/acquaintance rape.

Planning Part 2

☞ See "Planning Part 1" on page 62 for specific planning directions. Decide which activities will work best in same-gender groups, in age-level groups, or in either grouping.

☞ Include these topics in the second session:

* *Attitudes and perceptions*
* *How to prevent date/acquaintance rape or protect oneself in a potentially dangerous situation*
* *The absolute right to say no and be taken seriously*

☞ Make copies of the questionnaire that follows, and have pens and pencils available. Older youth will use this in the section "Investigate Stereotypes."

☞ Refer to the section "Where to Go for Help" beginning on page 90 for information on "What to Do in Case of Date/Acquaintance Rape."

Review the First Session

☞ Reread aloud the statements from "Why this is a youth issue," "What is date/acquaintance rape? or How a date turns into a crime," and "Findings and Facts About Rape" from the previous program "No Means No, Doesn't It?" Ask if there are any questions pertaining to the last session.

Investigate Stereotypes

☞ Form age-level groups.

For Younger Youth:

☞ Ask the youth to think of some things that females typically say and do. Then have the group members list things that males typically say and do. Record these comments on a chalkboard or on posterboard.

☞ Have several girls talk and act like boys. Invite several boys to imitate girls. Have the males respond to the females' perceptions of them, and ask the females to respond in kind.

☞ Be sensitive that stereotypes about boys tend to affirm strength whereas stereotypes about girls can feel degrading to them. Then discuss the following questions.

■ How did you feel watching stereotypes about your gender? Why do you think you felt that way? (You may want to ask these questions in same-sex groups first.)

■ Are males and females conditioned by society and by their peers to talk and act in certain ways? Give reasons or examples to support your answer.

■ Distribute copies of the questionnaire on page 67. Assure the youth that they don't have to have an opinion about every statement. Discuss the participants' responses and answer any questions they may have. Be aware that some of the youth's responses may be based on gossip and hearsay.

For Older Youth:

☞ Divide the group by gender and distribute copies of the questionnaire. Collect the group members' answer sheets and redistribute them, with the girls receiving the guy responses and vice versa.

☞ Give the youth a few minutes to review the responses, and then ask them to react to the answers. Have the gender groups discuss their reactions with the whole group.

☞ Address the concept of blame. Emphasize that the person who has been forced to have sex is not to be blamed.

☞ Discuss how peer pressure and sexual stereotypes influence the behavior of teens.

DO YOU AND YOUR FRIENDS SEE EYE TO EYE?

This exercise may help persons recognize sex-related stereotypes they unconsciously accept as true. Listed below are a number of generalizations, some of which are inaccurate. Place a *D* for disagree or an *A* for agree in front of each one. Your responses should reflect your honest opinions.

_____ 1. Girls who wear tight fitting or low-cut clothes are usually more willing to have sex than girls who dress more conservatively.

_____ 2. Boys have only one thing on their mind.

_____ 3. If a girl spends time at her boyfriend's house when she knows his parents aren't home, she is indicating that she is willing to have sex with him.

_____ 4. In a male/female relationship, girls need affection and companionship more than boys do.

_____ 5. The more sexually active a teenage male is, the more other guys look up to him.

_____ 6. If a boy spends a lot of money on a date, it is reasonable for him to expect the girl to show him some affection in return.

_____ 7. Girls never pressure their boyfriends for sex.

_____ 8. Many times, a girl says no to sex because she doesn't want to appear "easy"; but she doesn't really mean it.

_____ 9. Although it is now acceptable for girls to ask guys out on dates, boys worry a lot less about being rejected than girls do.

_____ 10. Males can't talk as openly about their feelings as females can.

Attitudes: What makes a man a man and a woman a woman?

Sometimes society seems to promote beliefs about "real men" and "real women" that you may or may not agree with. Put an "M" next to those behaviors that society says are more masculine, and an "F" next to those that you think society says are more feminine.

_____ gentle	_____ rebellious	_____ tough	_____ boisterous	_____ obedient
_____ quiet	_____ brave	_____ aggressive	_____ meek	_____ accepting
_____ nurturing	_____ intellegence	_____ cry easily	_____ show anger	_____ trust

_____ take initiative	_____ speak your mind, regardless	_____ wait to be asked
_____ don't make anyone mad	_____ be most attractive	_____ physically protect yourself
_____ learn to fight well	_____ find someone to protect you	_____ be stronger than everybody else

Gender Stereotypes and Rape

Do gender stereotypes make date/acquaintance rape easier to occur and ignore?

☞ Discuss with both age levels how date/acquaintance rape is most often suffered in silence because many people are confused about the messages that society gives them about who they are and how they should behave as males and females in relationships.

You may later want to emphasize that views are changing about women and men, but attitudes can take a long time to change, even after people may think that they ought to. You may find that some of your group members—or you yourself— believe in equality, but also believe in strict gender behaviors that make equality difficult.

☞ Ask the group to list some of the places these messages come from in society, such as school, church, parents, TV, and so on. Then discuss the following questions:

■ Why do you think that most sexual violence occurs against girls and women?

■ How does society view women? men? How do you view women? men? Why?

An Ounce of Prevention

Thinking through potential situations before they occur can make a difference in the outcome if the situation does in fact arise. Again form age-level groups in order to conduct the following roleplays.

For Younger Youth:
☞ Roleplay this scene: an adolescent who refuses a telephone request for a date from another youth (the caller may be either male or female). Afterward have the teens discuss these questions.

■ Why would a teenager refuse a date with someone?

■ Is it difficult to say no? Explain.

■ What are some conditions that would make you worry about a date or an outing with a member of the opposite sex?

For Older Youth:
☞ Divide these roleplay settings among the group members. Give each team time to perform its scenario, and then discuss the questions that follow.

1. A person coaxing his or her date to have sex

2. A male teenager responding to a buddy who is bragging about being ready to "score" on a date, no matter what

3. A teenage girl talking to a friend about the pressure her boyfriend is putting on her to have sex

■ Were these portrayals realistic? why or why not?

■ How seriously do you think your peers take the issue of date rape? Is it regarded as something that happens only to "other people"?

■ The act of rape is a felony. If someone you love were raped, would you consider the attacker a criminal? What if the attacker was your relative and the victim someone you don't know? Explain your response.

The Pound of Cure

☞ Bring the participants back together and ask them to brainstorm and record a list of possible ways to prevent date/acquaintance rape.

☞ Stimulate the discussion with examples of situations to avoid (single dates with someone you don't know; secluded places, including a home with no parents present; the use of alcohol and/or other drugs; dates with people who have a bad reputation). Also mention positive tactics such as group dating; going to places where there is an alternate way home if necessary; listening to one's friends and to trusted adults who express concerns about a choice of companion; being clear about one's own intentions and standards of behavior.

☞ Discuss the group members' list of preventive measures. Mention any significant methods that are not on the list.

☞ Have the participants rate their ideas and discuss why some methods will probably work better than others.

☞ Emphasize that the bottom line in preventing date rape is two-way communication, which means both saying no and hearing no.

What Does the Bible Say?

The story about the rape of Dinah in **Genesis 34:1-31** is similar to that of the rape of Tamar in **2 Samuel 13:1-39**. Apparently in each case the woman's father was more concerned about what was happening with his sons than with his daughter. The woman's brother or brothers came to her aid after the fact, each time to take revenge.

These accounts of rape and violence should be considered in light of the primary teaching of the Bible. Although the Old Testament contains calls by God to use military force to overthrow nations, the overwhelming message of the whole Bible is that it is never right to victimize or exploit another person, especially anyone considered less well equipped to resist that violence and oppression.

Emphasize how important the changes in beliefs about women as full human beings alters our understandings about rape as a crime against the woman.

☞ Read aloud **Genesis 34:1-31**. Review the main events of the story and discuss briefly the following questions.

■ Shechem "loved the girl, and spoke tenderly to her" after he raped her. Do you think that this episode qualifies as an expression of love by modern standards of conduct? Why or why not?

■ When Jacob found out what had happened, he was angry because his sons had made him look bad. They replied that their concern was for Dinah (verse 31). What do you think about their attitude and conduct?

☞ Refer to the previous discussions on cultural definitions of women and men's roles in society and point out that in Biblical times women were regarded *legally* as property of either fathers or husbands.

■ How might this belief have made rape be perceived as a crime primarily against the men?

☞ Read aloud the passage in **Samuel** or summarize it for the group. Then ask the participants to read **Galatians 5:16–6:10** and to discuss the following questions.

■ What are the behaviors and attitudes in both passages that are considered totally repugnant and sinful by the community of faith?

■ What actions and attitudes are appropriate and encourage the community of faith?

■ Does passion or the heat of the moment ever excuse abandoning one's religious principles? Explain your response.

■ Recall the last session's discussion of Jesus' teachings. What do you think Jesus Christ would think about date rape?

Worship

Sing or say together a hymn or song about acceptance.

Read aloud **Galatians 5:22-26**.

Gather in a circle for a time of prayer. Ask for prayer requests for persons who have experienced moments of weakness or fear in social settings. Point out that persons who do not want to say their requests or petitions aloud can just think about them. God will be aware of these concerns.

Pray silently, then together, the prayer that was posted during Part 1 of the previous session.

Patricia Reed lives in Alexandria, Virginia. She helps coordinate the Gleaning Network in the Washington, DC area and works with the Harvest of Hope program. Patty was a member of the design team for Forum '92 and was elected secretary of FAYM (Forum for Adults in Youth Ministry). As a Navy wife and mother of two teenagers, she has lived in ten cities coast to coast and has enjoyed a wide variety of church experiences. Patty has her own desktop publishing business and gets creative on her Macintosh computer and her weaving loom.

Laurel Schneider is currently pursuing her doctorate in theology at Vanderbilt University in Nashville, Tennessee. A native of Massachusetts, she received her M.Div. at Harvard and served a United Church of Christ parish in Cambridge, MA. She has contributed to several publications on issues of theology and society.

Coping With Death

by Allen Simons

PURPOSE: To help youth reflect on the emotional impact of death, to identify ways to discuss and cope with grief, and to reflect on the Scriptures and on the community of faith as primary resources for coping with death.

Preparation

☞ Make the three signs for the activity in "Reactions to Death." Write out key words on newsprint.

☞ Gather sheets of newsprint, paper, and pencils.

☞ Make copies of "Hints" and "Pitfalls" for the section "Practice Offering Sympathy" and of obituaries for the "Testimony" section.

☞ Make up puzzle pieces from cardboard or heavy paper for the activity in "Five Tasks to Heal Grief."

☞ Gather Bibles and commentaries on the following Scriptures. Print out the verses on a separate placard or poster:

Psalm 23:1, 4
Matthew 6:25-26
Mark 8:35
John 11:25a
John 11:25b-26
Romans 8:28
Romans 8:38-39
1 Corinthians 15:51, 52a, 53, 54b
Revelation 21:6b

Reactions to Death

When we hear that someone has died, we may experience surprise and shock, overwhelming sadness, or even relief. Or, we may not have strong feelings one way or the other. The following exercises will focus on the ways various circumstances and values can affect our feelings about the death of another person.

☞ **Before the session** write one or two key words from each of the statements below on a sheet of newsprint. Post the sheet after the exercise is completed.

☞ Place three signs around the room: "WOULD REACT STRONGLY," "WOULD REACT SOMEWHAT," and "WOULD NOT REACT STRONGLY."

☞ Read aloud each of the following statements, allowing time for the participants to move to the sign that best represents their feelings.

* Your grandfather has just died after a short illness. You were not that close to him.
* Your chemistry teacher is killed by a student he had reprimanded a few days ago.
* The evening news reports that people in Ethiopia are dying at the rate of one thousand persons a day.
* A teenager near your neighborhood is raped and beaten to death.
* You hear on the news that four hundred people have just died in an airplane crash.
* The father of a close friend dies suddenly.
* A US politician is assassinated.
* An acquaintance at your school commits suicide.
* You hear a news report that a homeless person was found dead near a freeway in your town.
* Your cousin is killed in a drive-by shooting.

☞ Discuss these questions.
■ Which statements created the strongest feelings? Why?

■ When is death hardest to understand? Why?

■ What makes death difficult to cope with?

■ How are your feelings about a specific death affected by the circumstances surrounding it?

■ How does your response to the death reflect your values? (Some may feel a greater sense of loss if the deceased person was young and had great potential than if the person was older and had already had a chance to contribute to society.)

■ What makes someone or something feel close to us?

■ Should we respond differently to the death of those who are close to us than we do to those we were not personally involved with? Why, or why not?

Getting Through Grief

When people confront the reality of their own impending death or the death of someone close to them, they begin a grieving process. Grieving is a natural transition period during which persons begin to deal with a potential loss or a loss that has already occurred. Dr. Elisabeth Kübler-Ross has described this process (see the sidebar "Stages of Grief") in her book *On Death and Dying* (Macmillan Publishing Company, 1969). The stages are essentially the same for the person who is dying and the persons who will grieve their death.

☞ Have the participants form small groups.

☞ Use the information in the sidebar to talk about the five stages of grief. Discuss them briefly.

☞ Ask each group to choose one of the stages of grief to pantomime for the total group. Allow fifteen minutes for the participants to work on their pantomime.

☞ Have each small group present its pantomime to the total group. The others should try to identify that particular stage of grief.

Help From the Bible

Viewing a personal loss through the lens of faith is a primary way to work through grief.

☞ Have small groups each select three passages from the Scripture placards that were prepared earlier and determine which Scripture most closely reflects their group's beliefs and concerns about death.

☞ Have each group design a human sculpture that represents the members' beliefs about death and then present it to the whole group. (A human sculpture uses persons to construct a "frozen" image that represents a particular idea or concept.)

☞ Discuss the insights that the participants gained from the Scriptures and from the living sculptures.

Stages of Grief

First Stage: Denial and Isolation: The person refuses to accept his or her own impending death. He or she pretends that nothing has changed, but may withdraw from most social contact.

Second Stage: Anger: As the fact of death becomes more real, the person becomes angry and feels the injustice of it all.

Third Stage: Bargaining: As the person attempts to regain control, she or he may try to strike a bargain with God (for example, "If I am allowed to live, I will dedicate the rest of my life to good works.")

Fourth Stage: Depression: As the reality of one's death can no longer be avoided, the person feels helpless and becomes deeply depressed.

Fifth Stage: Acceptance: Realizing his or her inability to avoid death, the person comes to a kind of acceptance of death and claims some inner peace.

Practice Offering Sympathy

☞ Remain in small groups and designate a leader in each one. Distribute copies of the "Pitfalls" and "Hints" from page 72.

☞ Ask two persons in each group to roleplay a situation in which one is grieving and the other is trying to offer consolation. In the first part of the conversation, the "helper" is to fall prey to some of the "pitfalls" listed in the sidebar.

☞ Stop the action and ask the other group members to identify any pitfalls that they observed. Then ask the roleplayers to begin again, using the helpful hints. Stop and identify the positive approaches.

☞ The small-group leaders will then ask someone who has experienced a death to comment on the experience while other group members offer sympathy using some of the helpful hints. Begin with the death of a pet and continue with the death of a friend or relative. (No one should feel any pressure to participate in any segment of this exercise.)

Pitfalls to Avoid
When Discussing Death

* Using language that invites denial: "She's just sleeping," "God needed him," "She's on a long journey."

* Doing too much of the talking whether you are expressing your own faith or dealing with some other issue.

* Asking insensitive questions: "What was the real cause of his death?" "How can you keep from crying?" "Is it true that your marriage was in trouble then?"

* Passing judgment on the grieving person's emotions: "How can you feel angry toward your mother after all that she did for you?"

* Presuming to know the other person's reactions: "You must be utterly devastated by your dad's death!" "I know that you will miss her. She was so sweet."

* Making promises or giving assurances that are not under your control: "Once you get past the first year, you will feel much better."

Hints for Helping
Bereaved Persons

* Get in touch with your own feelings about the experience.

* Listen carefully and sympathetically to the other person's feelings.

* Accept the other person's emotions without passing judgment.

* Help the person explore his or her feelings.

* Use factual and straightforward language.

* Share your feelings when appropriate and natural.

* Allow the person to set his or her own limits.

* Talk about your own sense of faith and hope when it would be appropriate and not intrusive.

* Say "I don't know" when that is the case.

Two Big Questions

The following questions often come to mind in the aftermath of death: (1) Why do people we care about die? (2) Why do they die before they or we are ready to say good-bye?

Throughout history philosophers, theologians, scientists, sages, and ordinary people have tried to find an answer to these painful questions. No one answer is totally satisfactory in all cases. Each person needs to search for answers that are meaningful and comforting to her or him.

☞ Post the two questions in the first paragraph.

☞ Ask the participants to react to the questions in small groups. After five minutes, bring everyone back together for a summary of the group's responses.

Testimony of a Community
of Faith

Following a person's death, usually a notice called an obituary appears in the local newspapers. These death notices are interesting for the details they include and sometimes for the facts they omit.

☞ Look over the death notices in the local paper or in one or more issues of a news magazine. If you can, obtain from the library photocopies of one or more obituaries from the 1920's or 30's. Distribute them to the group members.

☞ Ask the group members to recall or count the euphemisms in the old obituary. (A euphemism is a milder word or phrase that is substituted for a more direct term.) Ask the participants to call out the "translation" of each euphemism they can identify.

☞ Compare the recent death notices with the old one. Ask for several volunteers to read aloud their obituary and then discuss the following questions.

■ Why do we use euphemisms to refer to death?

■ Why is death often considered a taboo subject?

■ What does the old obituary reveal about the persons who died? What do you think it says about the one who wrote it?

■ How do you think people in an earlier time felt about death?

■ How do you personally feel about death? What terms related to death do you feel comfortable using?

- What, do you think, does the writer of the obituary believe about life? about death?

- How does the community of faith of which the deceased was a member react to death?

- Does this obituary illustrate a measure of denial about illness or death?

- What does our current community of faith believe about death and life? How do you know?

☞ Distribute a blank piece of paper and a pen or pencil to each participant. Ask everyone to spend five minutes writing her or his own obituary. The group members are to imagine the date of their death, and think of what things they would like to have written about them in an obituary. Ask for volunteers to read aloud their death notice.

Five Tasks to Heal Grief

When we have suffered a loss, we have to work through the stages of grief to get our lives back together. Some people get stuck in a stage and have a hard time moving on. Even though it is hard, we need to do several things to keep going. The first is acceptance of the loss, followed by "processing." Processing includes talking out feelings, making meaning of what has happened, and making realistic decisions about what is next in life. Throughout this processing, we need the help and support of others, especially those who have experienced something similar.

☞ Have the group members put together the decision/action puzzle pieces. When the puzzle is complete, talk about how these activities can help someone who is working though grief. (Note that too many changes at the same time can be as problematic as getting stuck.)

Puzzle Pieces:
☞ Identify a project that you can support in the name of the deceased person.
☞ Establish a memorial fund in the name of the deceased.
☞ Record positive remembrances.
☞ Identify persons or groups that could benefit from the deceased person's belongings.
☞ Begin new personal activities or renew old ones.
☞ Begin new relationships, with care.
☞ Take a vacation.
☞ Begin an exercise program.
☞ Visit someone you have not seen in a long time.
☞ Go back to familiar activities.

Have a Panel Discussion

Optional: Funeral practices vary from community to community, from place to place, and from culture to culture. A panel discussion would broaden the conversation about how funerals are conducted and how they help people deal with grief. Include persons who represent all or most of the racial and cultural groups in your community. Ask the panel members to discuss funeral practices, ways of dealing with grief, how the community is involved in healing, and how they personally use and understand Scripture in coping with grief.

Worship

Sing or recite the words to "Hymn of Promise" (*The United Methodist Hymnal,* No. 707) or other resurrection hymn or song.

Say to the group members: "Learning to cope with our own death or that of another is a process of acceptance and of the development of hope. How can we hope when we know that death awaits us all? If we remember that in the dormant seed of death there can be found the seed of new life and resurrection, our hope is reborn."

Read together a prayer of hope from the funeral liturgy, such as the one on page 871 or 872 of the *Hymnal.*

Pray together. Ask the group members to sit on the floor in a circle and hold hands. Invite a volunteer to begin with a short prayer sentence, and then to squeeze the hand of the next person, who will continue with his or her own prayer or pass by squeezing the next person's hand. Go around the circle.

Sing or say "O God, Our Help in Ages Past" (*The United Methodist Hymnal,* No. 117).

From Directions in Faith/JJA, page 26
© 1994 by Cokesbury.

Allen Simons is associate council director of the Rocky Mountain Annual Conference and works in the area of youth ministry, camping, and the General Board of Discipleship. He enjoys camping, hiking, photography, and music. Al lives in Colorado Springs with his wife, Lynne Coffman, who is a United Methodist pastor and who shares in discussing and contributing ideas for his writing.

How Do I Cope With Dangerous Classmates?

by Martha Maxham and Diana Hynson

PURPOSE: To help youth understand the role they can play in helping to create a peaceful environment at their school, while at the same time considering their own personal safety.

Background

Many junior, middle, and senior high school students in our society confront potentially dangerous situations or classmates at school on a daily basis. This session will help teens take a look at how they can and should respond to threatening situations they may encounter. Stress throughout this program that the youth must think of their own safety first. Few situations warrant the risk of getting hurt (or worse) for the sake of looking like a hero.

See also the article "Living With Fear" beginning on page 26.

Draw Your School

☞ Group participants in clusters of three or four according to the school they attend.

☞ Distribute crayons or markers and poster paper to each person. Ask the group members to draw a picture, collage, or other representation of how they see their school. They should use colors that describe their feelings and experiences (for example: orange and yellow for warmth, blue for sad, green for growth, and so forth).

☞ Have the group members draw two more symbols on the school poster that represent home and church. The size and depiction of home and church should correspond to their importance compared to school.

☞ Give each group a chance to explain their picture. Tape the artwork to the meeting room walls for the duration of the program.

Them's Fightin' Words!

The reasons for violent behavior are many and varied, but violent behavior is learned. Some children learn lessons in violence from their earliest years through dysfunctional or abusive parenting. Others are coached, educated, and encouraged to resolve issues aggressively, as if a more moderate approach is sissified or unseemly. Some persons learn aggression because the people who influence them are ignorant in ways of peace. The media is often a major influence in teaching and reinforcing the message that violence is the preferred option for problem-solving.

No matter what else is true, violence surely does not happen in a vacuum. At school, the usual pattern is for a dispute (however silly) to start; escalate with taunts, insults, or other negative impetus; draw up sides; and then, literally sometimes, push comes to shove and violence erupts. The best way to avoid violence in school is to stop it before it starts. Violence does not have to happen. There are other choices.

☞ Write on a chalkboard or posted newsprint two or three examples of transitional statements that push a disagreement into a fight, such as
* "Are you going to let her get away with that?"
* "Did you hear what that creep called you?"
* "You don't have to take that stuff from him."

☞ Distribute markers. Use the chalkboard or paper as a graffiti board and invite group members to add as many examples as they can in five or six minutes. Add others later if they come up. Put a different number or letter by each example.

☞ Post more newsprint and ask for a nonviolent alternative comment for every example on the graffiti board, such as:
* "It's no big deal; let her do it if she wants."
* "I think you're okay; don't let that kind of talk bother you."
* "You can rise above that stuff. Leave it be."

☞ Debrief for a few minutes. Keep these posters for another activity.

Good News

☞ Form small, age-level groups of two to four persons and assign each group one or more of the following Bible passages. Use all of them. Provide Bibles, commentaries, newsprint, and markers.

☞ Each group is to read its Bible verse or passage, study what it means, and then write on the newsprint a newspaper headline that summarizes the content. Tape the headline papers to the wall.

☞ Assign to *younger youth*
Ecclesiastes 11:9-10
Matthew 5:9
Luke 22:47-53
Colossians 3:15-17

☞ Assign to *older youth*
Matthew 5:38-42
Matthew 25:31-46
Romans 7:14-17, 21–8:1
Ephesians 6:10-17

☞ After the headlines are done, ask someone to read aloud **Matthew 5:38-48**. Follow the reading of this familiar Scripture passage with some questions for group discussion:

■ What is the Christian response to a specific instance of evil?

■ What does it mean to "turn the other cheek"?

■ When should you turn the other cheek?

■ How long should a teen turn the other cheek while being bullied or threatened in some way?

■ How do we deal with the fact that violent behavior is sometimes ignored or condoned, and that some persons never seem to suffer the consequences of their actions?

Good News: You Don't Have to Fight!

This activity will draw together the points from each of the preceding activities to help group members examine the benefits and tactics for avoiding fights.

☞ Review the main points of the Scripture readings, the "diffusing" comments to "fightin' words," and the comments and images of the various schools from the first activity.

☞ Using the reports from participants' own school experiences of fights or other violence, in pairs or triads practice fight stopping tactics.

☞ Debrief the exercise by discussing the following questions.

■ What fueled the fight or violence? Why?

■ What defused it? Why?

■ How did you feel about avoiding or defusing violence?

■ What response did you get from your peers? Was it helpful or not? Why?

---

*"You have heard that it was said,
'You shall love your neighbor and hate your enemy.'
But I say to you: Love your enemies
and pray for those who persecute you . . .
For if you love those who love you
what reward do you have?
Do not even the tax collectors do the same?
And if you greet only your brothers and sisters,
what more are you doing than others?*

Matthew 5:43-44; 46-47a

When the Going Gets Rough

The activities so far have addressed situations of coping with aggressive behavior. What happens when that aggression gets dangerous? The purpose of this activity is to zero in on how Christian teens can deal with dangerous situations that they may have to confront at their schools.

☞ Divide into small groups and give a copy of the following questions to each group.

■ What would you do if you were in each situation?

■ How would or should a Christian respond to this or a similar situation?

■ What other options might work? Why?

■ What other tactics should you avoid? Why?

☞ Using one of the following situations or one from their own experience, have small groups discuss the four questions, then compose a brief skit to present the assigned situation and its resolution.

1. *The Locker*

You go to your locker earlier than usual one morning. As you are reaching for some books, you can't help but notice that the student who has the locker next to yours is casually placing a handgun in his locker. He sees your shocked stare and says, "Hey, just keep cool about this and everything will be okay. Make a noise about it and you'll find yourself staring down the barrel of this baby!" What will you do?

2. *The Delivery*

Your best friend desperately needs money. He has recently lost his job at The Burger Palace and his father is also unemployed. There isn't much you can do to help out. At lunch one day he tells you that after school he is going to help out a new friend by delivering a small bag of crack to a phone booth not far from your school. He tries to explain: "It's just once, and it's a lot of money." You beg your friend not to make the delivery, knowing that his new "friend" is one of the leaders of a drug ring at the school. That "friend" sees the two of you talking in the cafeteria and may assume you know something you shouldn't. Now what do you do?

3. *The Game*

During a basketball game at school one evening, you step out of the gym to get a drink at the water fountain. You see a group of students you don't know very well sneaking toward the computer lab, so you follow them to see what's up. You soon discover that the youth apparently plan to vandalize the lab. When you protest, they call you a wimp and threaten to beat you up if you don't join in the "fun." What will you do?

4. *The Dance*

Outside in the parking lot during a school-sponsored dance, you accidentally witness the beating of a junior high student by a gang of older students. As you are running toward the school to get help, you suddenly feel a hand on your shoulder and a knife at your back. Someone whispers in a menacing tone, "If you tell anyone what you just saw, your next three years at this school will be pure hell." What will you do?

5. *The Fight*

Your family is far from wealthy. As a consequence, you have a modest wardrobe. You make do with hand-me-downs, and you don't really mind. For the past two weeks, however, you have been taunted by a group of students who stand outside the school every afternoon as you leave. They have been making derogatory remarks about you and your family. You know that these students are members of a very rough clique at your school. So far you have just ignored them, but it is becoming harder to do so. Your friends want you to challenge them to a fight. You don't feel comfortable with this idea, but now your best friend informs you that your group has challenged this other group to a fight after school today. You know your friends are coming to your aid because they care about you, but you don't want to be the cause of a confrontation. In one hour the final school bell will ring. What will you do?

To Whom Can You Turn?

☞ Say to the group members (still in the small groups and after the presentation of their scenarios): "If you really had to confront one of the above situations, do you think your parents or teachers would sympathize with your predicament and would understand this kind of danger?"

☞ Then ask the youth to list some people they would feel comfortable turning to for help when faced with threatening situations (parents, teachers, pastors, youth group advisers, and so forth).

Where Do We Go From Here?

If during this session you find out that a number of the group members do regularly confront dangerous situations at school, discuss some ways to aid these youth. Ask for suggestions as to how your church can be of help. Some possible options:

▶ Form a support group consisting of the pastor, several teens, and a school representative.

▶ Arrange a meeting between some members of the school board and some of the church members, including both parents and youth.

▶ Set up a "big brother" and/or "big sister" program within the youth group in order to help younger teens who are just entering junior or senior high.

Sometimes we don't know how to deal with frightening or intimidating situations. Some of our classmates at school endanger themselves and others by their actions. We often find it hard to respond with Christian love to a negative or threatening attitude or deed.

Worship

Begin the worship period by singing "Dona Nobis Pacem" (*The United Methodist Hymnal,* No. 376) or another hymn or song about peace.

Distribute slips of paper and pencils or pens to the group members. Ask them to think of a dangerous situation at school they or someone they know is facing or has faced in the past. Have them write the situation on the slip of paper (if the threat involves a particular student or group of students, they may list the name or names). Then pass around a basket to collect the slips of paper. (Destroy the slips after the worship period.)

Pray this prayer: "O God, sometimes we don't know how to deal with frightening or intimidating situations, such as the ones we now offer up to you. Some of our classmates at school endanger themselves and others by their actions. We often find it hard to respond with Christian love to a negative or threatening attitude or deed. Watch over us when we face danger and even violence. Above all, enable us to convey a spirit of peace in a world that often promotes conflict."

Close the worship by singing "Let There Be Peace on Earth" (*The United Methodist Hymnal,* No. 431)

Martha Knobel Maxham is a diaconal minister of education. She has a Master of Christian Education from Scarritt College in Nashville, Tennessee. Martha has served churches in the Virginia and Baltimore-Washington annual conferences of The United Methodist Church. Presently she is working as the Director of Christian Education at Chevy Chase United Methodist Church near Washington, DC.

Diana L. Hynson is an editor with the Department of Youth Publications at The United Methodist Publishing House in Nashville, TN. Diana has edited and contributed to several youth publications.

Loving Beyond Hate

by David P. Harris

PURPOSE: To help youth explore the issue of hatred and examine ways the gospel calls us to respond to hate.

Holy Hypotheses

Harboring hatred is at least partly the result of fear, ignorance, intolerance, and an inability to forgive. The idea of forgiving again and again, which **Matthew 18:21-22** urges, seems foreign to many people. That fear is the opposite of love, or that "perfect love casts out fear" (**1 John 4:18-21**), dawns slowly in our thinking. Also, the true test of our love for God is that we will love our "brothers and sisters."

Love Defeats Hate

Prepare by collecting twice as many magazine pictures as the number of group members (each picture should include at least two persons). Read **Matthew 18:21-22** and **1 John 4:18-21**.

Be ready to read and summarize the key points in those Scriptures: Jesus illustrates the necessity and importance of forgiving others and reminds us that God's mercy is central to the concept of forgiveness (**Matthew 18:23-35**). If God can love and forgive humankind, we must surely be forgiving in our relationships with others. Emphasize that perfect love, which flows from God and which casts out fear, is meant to work in our life as we love those around us (**1 John 4:18-21**).

☞ Ask the participants to form pairs, and have each group member select one of the magazine pictures from the collection you have provided. The partners will take turns telling each other how the picture they selected might show intolerance and hatred or forgiveness and love. Allow several minutes.

☞ Form new groups of three or four persons. Instruct each group to link their pictures together by creating a new story about forgiveness or love. They can combine their ideas from the first story or make up an entirely new story. Urge the youth to be creative.

☞ Ask these questions:
■ How many times was forgiveness necessary? Was the forgiven person hard to love? If so, why?

■ Who in your story or picture was filled with hate?

■ What person or persons in your story or picture do you identify with the most? Why?

Hate: Up Close and Personal

Facing up to hate is a challenge to our faith and our honesty. Sometimes we are tempted to say we don't see much evidence of hate in our everyday life; but if we read the newspaper or watch TV news broadcasts, attend school, or go out in public at all, we see hate in action.

The following examples illustrate hate and its close relatives, prejudice and injustice, which are a part of our own life, sometimes as close as our own school, community, church, or family. If we recognize ourselves in any of these situations, we must look to Jesus' example for aid in doing something to get rid of the fear and hate, and in replacing our fearfulness with love.

One immediate response is to think *theologically*, that is, to ask, What would God have me do as a faithful and loving disciple? A follow-up step is to act on what one's faith suggests.

Have you seen or heard
■ a person treated differently because of his or her skin color?

■ someone making fun of another person?

■ a group loudly proclaiming, "We're right and they're wrong!"? (Think about hot issues like abortion, public education, or civil rights that crop up almost daily in the media.)

■ two racial groups always sitting at separate tables in the school cafeteria?

■ a friend referring to another human being as "they"?

■ a parent saying, "It's best to date, or make friends with, your own kind"?

■ a person being verbally or physically harassed because of his or her sexual orientation, real or presumed?

■ someone ignored or treated poorly because of limitations in her or his physical, mental, emotional, or social capabilities?

☞ Use the following suggestions as discussion or roleplay starters, or develop your own. Ask for volunteers to use the biblical principles you studied earlier to act out ways to deal lovingly, not only with persons who are the victims of hatred, but with the victimizers as well.

1. A male teen wearing two hearing aids is obviously missing most of a conversation in the noisy hallway between classes and finally asks someone to repeat what he or she said. One of the other teens responds in a sarcastic tone of voice, "What's the matter? You *deaf*, or something?"

2. A female teenager is one of a few persons in her school who belong to a certain religious group. Several of the older male students are taunting her by chanting a slang characterization that demeans her religious affiliation. Other students, who are supposed to be her friends, are silent.

3. A male student who is quiet and usually keeps to himself finds the word *queer* written in permanent marker all over his locker.

4. A female teen from a racial or an ethnic group that is a numerical minority in her community tells her best friend that she has been asked out by someone from the racial or ethnic majority. The friend makes a scornful reply. (You can also switch the majority/minority roles.)

5. Two or three students are gossiping and laughing, sharing stereotypical negative comments about "them," when you notice that a teen from that group of "them" has heard the whole conversation. (You can also leave out the teen's overhearing the remarks and respond to the comments on their own merit.)

Hate's Hot

The examples so far are about "legally tolerable" hate or prejudice. When a person is confronted because of race, nationality, sexual orientation, physical or mental disability, or gender, and is the victim of assault, aggravated assault, battery, vandalism, robbery, mob action, telephone harassment, or disorderly conduct, the victimizer has crossed the line from ignorance, stupidity, and cruelty to a legal misdemeanor or felony. These actions are hate crimes.

Hate crimes are on the rise and are increasingly more violent. A sizable number of these crimes are committed by persons under age eighteen— about 42% in Chicago, for instance. Consider the following incidents:

▶ A Detroit lesbian couple was shot and killed in their front yard in 1992 by a 65-year-old next door neighbor, who had harassed them for 25 years.

▶ A 29-year-old Jewish scholar was stabbed to death by a group of young rioters during unrest in Brooklyn's Crown Heights in August 1991, following the tragic accidental death of a black child by a Jewish driver.

▶ An African American gay man was attacked in his apartment by two African American acquaintances who tied him to a chair and threw him off the balcony. Somehow he survived.

▶ A reputed white supremacist and Third Reich fanatic located a doctor's name in the Yellow pages, made an appointment, and when his turn came to see the doctor, shot him four times in the chest. The plastic surgeon was a white Gentile, but the killer's apparent motive was that persons like the doctor "destroy the white race by tricking Aryans into breeding with the wrong race by giving non-Aryans Nordic features."*

*The final incident was reported by *Newsweek*, August 23, 1993; page 32. The others were compiled through the Chicago Lawyers' Committee for Civil Rights Under Law, Inc., Project to Combat Bias Violence.

☞ Divide the group into four small groups and assign each group a different incident. Ask them to decide if the crime is a hate crime and to be prepared to tell why it is or is not.

☞ Then discuss the following questions.

■ What feelings does the situation elicit? Why?

■ What do you think motivates someone to commit a hate crime?

■ If a mob gets "carried away" and persons in that crowd commit a hate crime, who is responsible? Why do you think so?

■ If a Christian killed another Christian in the name of God and because of his or her Christianity, would that be a hate crime? Why or why not? Suppose both persons are of the same race and the crime is motivated by race? Is that action defensible? Why or why not?

Hooked On Hate

Who are the groups that hate other people? Some of these people and groups are highly visible, such as the *Ku Klux Klan*. The KKK considers people who are not light- or white-skinned to be inferior. *Neo-Nazis* revive the prejudices of Hitler's Germany and the claim of superiority for people of Aryan (Indo-European) heritage. Nazi prejudice extended not only to Jewish persons, but also to homosexual persons, people of African heritage, Gypsies, persons with handicapping conditions, and others. Some *Skinhead* groups are kindred spirits, believing also that people who do not conform to the "ideal" of so-called "superior" physical characteristics, race, culture, and so on, are subject at the very least to scorn and possibly to harassment, injury, or even murder.

But hate-mongers do not have to belong to an organized group. Hate crimes can be acts of "opportunity" as well as intentional, when, for example two guys discover that a third male is gay and beat him up. These persons live in our neighborhoods and work in our communities. They look like you and me, but they hate whole groups of other human beings and mistakenly believe that those persons are less valuable than they are.

Any of us may be guilty of hating others. The Japan-bashing that erupts from time to time in the US is one example. Of course, it is acceptable to care for the concerns of one's own nation; but indiscriminately vilifying everyone in another culture doesn't live up to Jesus' standard of being a loving neighbor.

One can easily see how such hate groups do not fit Jesus' call to love our neighbor (**Leviticus 19:18; Luke 10:25-37**). When individuals or a group of people claim superiority on the basis of nationality, race, skin color, religious belief, physical and mental ability, gender, or sexual orientation, we must ask, "Is this person or group acting out of hate?"

Breaking Hate's Hold

Transforming hate and injustice into something good takes God's power, first of all; and then it requires our faith and action. Affirming the power of love to win over hate and fear is the first step. That means we won't fight hate with hate. Hate, revenge, and violence never accomplish anything positive or loving; they always lead to more hate, revenge, and violence. What's needed is a plan that puts love into action. You and your group members have just practiced some ways to do this on an immediate, personal level. Now consider deeper levels.

☞ Brainstorm a list of possibilities for addressing hate or prejudice-based violence in your community, including your own group, if necessary.

Some possibilities for group action:
▶ inviting a guest who knows about hate groups and hate crimes to speak to the church or your group

▶ taking an "observational survey" at local schools for how much violence is motivated by hate and making a presentation to school administrators

▶ studying peacemaking and forgiveness

▶ designing a bulletin board to teach about breaking hate's hold

▶ writing to prominent people (your bishop or other church leaders, congresspersons, other local and national leaders) to learn their views and to express your own

☞ Ask the participants to pick an item from the list of suggestions that represents something they may want to do on their own. (It's all right to add new ideas at this point.) Get updates on these personal projects at your next meeting.

☞ Now let the group choose one idea for a project. After the project has been chosen, pick a small committee to be responsible for reminding the group members of their project, and for planning dates and deadlines and any other details that may be vital to the success of your goal: learning to replace hate with love.

Worship

Love is the Scripture's response to hate. In closing this session, emphasize the power of a loving response.

Ask five volunteers to read aloud these portions of **1 Corinthians 13:1-13**: verses 1-3, verses 4-7, verses 8-10, verses 11-12, and verse 13.

Invite the group members to join in singing or reciting the following "Love" round, to the tune of "Hi, Ho, Nobody Home":

> Love, love, love, love,
> Christians, this is your call;
> Love your neighbor as yourself
> For God loves all.

An alternate version for the second line of the "Love" round is, "The gospel in a word is love." Sing the song through several times, and then try it as a round.

Conclude the worship period with the prayer that follows (or write one of your own): "O God, teach us to love all people, both individuals and groups. May we use your redeeming, transforming love to overcome the hatreds that plague our world. Give us the courage to face our own fear and hatred, as we claim for ourselves the life-changing love of Christ. **Amen.**"

David P. Harris is a pastor who loves to teach, because in teaching there is an opportunity to know God and to help others in knowing God. David's second love is play—play as a musician, a clown, a husband, a father, and a child of God—for play is the soil of prayer and the fertilizer for God's work. David's primary belief in the power of God to give meaning to life and to transform life with Christ's love motivates his teaching, his learning, his playing, his writing, and perhaps most of all his pastoring of a congregation. Dave and his family live in Pennsylvania.

> *"O God, teach us to love all people,*
> *both individuals and groups.*
> *May we use your redeeming,*
> *transforming love*
> *to overcome the hatreds that plague our world.*
> *Give us the courage to face*
> *our own fear and hatred,*
> *as we claim for ourselves*
> *the life-changing love of Christ. Amen."*

Nonviolence: A Valuable Alternative

by Wendy Downing-Birdwell

PURPOSE: To make youth more aware of the violence that permeates our culture and to encourage them to embrace nonviolence in conflict resolution, recreational activities, and entertainment.

Preparation

This event is designed to be an overnight retreat, in a setting that differs from routine surroundings. The aim of the Friday-night activities is to help youth become aware of the subtle ways that violence invades our culture and to help them see the need for nonviolent alternatives in everyday living. On Saturday, the activities will be geared toward practicing nonviolence in conflict resolution.

☞ Make sure the planning team includes at least two or three youth along with adult sponsors.

☞ Decide when and where the retreat will be held, and advertise the retreat (and its purpose) at least one month in advance. You need access and transportation to a local mall.

☞ Each activity has a suggested time; adjust it according to the interest and ability level of your group. Be sure to schedule time for breaks, meal preparation and clean up, recreation, and travel.

☞ Gather the supplies and equipment you will need for the scavenger hunt, snacks, devotional, peace bags, media inventory, and worship.

Friday Night Activities

Violence-Around-Me Scavenger Hunt (60 minutes)

This activity is to take place at a shopping mall on the way to the retreat location.

☞ Ask the youth to form teams of no more than five persons. Give each team a pad of paper and a pencil. Make sure at least one member of each small group has a watch.

☞ Give the group members about forty-five minutes to look around the mall and write down all the items they see that have some connection to violence. (The examples can include anything from movies being shown at the theaters to military toys in the stores.) **Remind them that they are not shopping, they are hunting!**

☞ The discussion of the hunt will take place at the retreat location later in the evening. Set a certain time and place to regroup. When everyone arrives at the designated meeting place, collect the note pads and continue on to the retreat location.

Scavenger Hunt Discussion (30-45 minutes)

☞ After settling in at the retreat site, get out the note pads used in the scavenger hunt and have the youth divide into the same teams they formed at the mall.

☞ Distribute the note pads to the respective teams. Invite a spokesperson from each group to read aloud the items on its list.

☞ Designate someone to be the "judge" to determine whether every item on the list is actually "violent." The team that listed the most examples of "violence around me" is the winner of the hunt.

☞ Lead a discussion about the scavenger hunt with the following questions:

■ Were you surprised by any of the examples of violence you found on the hunt?

■ Were you surprised by how *many* examples you found?

■ Were you surprised by how many items you found that were designed for use by children and youth?

■ Why do you think our society tolerates so much violence in so many areas of our life?

■ What can we do about such an ingrained problem?

"Nonviolent" Snacks (30 minutes)

Provide doughnuts, brownies, cookies, or cupcakes for snacks. Make flags out of toothpicks and paper, and write on each flag a quotation having to do with peace, war, violence, or love. Place a flag in each snack. Some suggested quotations:

▶ "Love rules without a sword, love binds without a cord"—Anonymous

▶ "There never was a good war or a bad peace"—Benjamin Franklin

▶ "Perseverance is more prevailing than violence"—Plutarch

▶ "Love, and do what you like"—St. Augustine

▶ "A day of battle is a day of harvest for the devil"—William Hook

▶ "Violence defeats its own ends"—William Hazlitt

▶ "A good portion of the evils that afflict mankind is due to the erroneous belief that life can be made secure by violence"—Leo Tolstoy

Devotional (15 minutes)

Read aloud a newspaper clipping that describes some kind of violence that has taken place in your community in the past week. Then pass around a wet, unfolded handkerchief that has mud on it so that each person who touches it gets dirt on his or her hands.

Say: "Our hands are symbolically dirty because of our sinful human nature that leads to all instances of violence in our world." Ask each person to complete this sentence: "One way that I participate in violence is . . ."

After everyone has made a confession, use a damp cloth (or several wet paper towels) to clean each person's hands as a sign of forgiveness and pardon. As you are passing around the damp cloth, say: "God will guide us in the ways of peace."

Close the devotional time with a prayer.

Saturday Activities

Peace Is My "Bag" (30 minutes)

Violence comes at us from every direction and is so prevalent in our culture that we can easily become desensitized to its existence. This retreat is a chance to "bombard" the group members with the concept of nonviolence in every way possible.

☞ Provide a paper lunch sack for each person. Ask the youth to decorate the bags with something that symbolizes peace and/or nonviolence for them (for example, two clasped hands, a smiling face, a peaceful landscape, a head bowed in prayer).

☞ Provide decorating supplies such as cotton balls, material scraps, paints, markers, and glue. When the bags are finished, hang them on a wall in a central location.

☞ Periodically during the retreat (before or after each meal and each activity) secretly place "Nonviolent Reminders" in the bags.

Sample "Nonviolent Reminders"

▶ Bookmarks with the Beatitudes printed on them (see **Matthew 5**)

▶ A scroll (tied) containing a special message

▶ Cookies in the shape of a lamb or a peace symbol

▶ Plastic swords (like those used in appetizers) with a printed version of **Matthew 26:52** tied to them

▶ A cutout of a coat printed with **Luke 6:29**

▶ A "fan" made of slips of colored paper. Punch a hole in all the slips, and hold them together with a bread tie. Print a "peace psalm" on each separate slip (**Psalm 4:8; 29:11; 34:14; 85:8; 119:165**).

Media Inventory (45-60 minutes)

☞ Set up four learning centers in a large room. Form four to eight teams.

☞ *Learning Center 1: Print media.* Display newspapers and magazines along with pieces of posterboard, glue, and scissors. Provide a list of topics (Violence and Children, Violence and TV, Symbols of Nonviolence, and so forth). Have each small group choose a topic and construct a collage using clippings from newspapers and pictures from magazines. (Several groups may work at this center at the same time.)

☞ *Learning Center 2: News.* Have a TV and a VCR set up with pretaped news clips (local or national) that show some sort of violence. Have the youth discuss and record their answers to the following question after they have viewed the clips:

■ How would your response to the violence and the victim or victims involved be different if the event you just saw happened in your state? in your neighborhood? to your family?

☞ *Learning Center 3: TV and movies.* Have available at least two rented videotapes of violent movies and at least one videotape clip that shows violence in a TV show. Be sure you have permission to show a copyrighted film. Indicate the segment of the movie you would like the youth to watch using the number counter on the VCR (not more than five to eight minutes per set segment). Have the groups discuss and record their answers to the following questions and statements:

■ Why are these films and TV shows so popular?

■ In what ways do you think a continual dose of this kind of media violence affects one's behavior?

☞ *Learning Center 4: Music.* Have on display printed song lyrics or a cassette player along with tapes of some popular songs that seem to promote violence. (Before the event get suggestions of current song titles from the youth.) Have the groups discuss and answer the following questions after reading or listening to the lyrics:

■ What is the appeal of this kind of music?

■ Do you feel that buying music with violent lyrics says anything about our own tolerance of violence?

☞ *Regroup.* After all the groups have been to every center, call everyone back together to discuss any answers the groups recorded that they would like to bring to the entire group. Ask for explanations of the collages.

Teen Mediation and Nonviolent Problem Solving

Teen violence is often a result of teens who feel powerless seizing the power that is available to them—being tougher than the "other guy," doing to you before you do to me, retaliating more forcefully than the original action (which just escalates the problem), obtaining a bigger and better weapon. Children who have been violated, especially by adults who have ALL the power, may later grow to be violent teens.

In any argument (as well as before an argument) everyone has a position (what I want) and an interest (why I want it). Nonviolent problem solving concentrates on trying to find a win-win solution that understands and accommodates to each party's position and interest. A dispute that turns into a fight, with or without violence, is at best a win-lose situation. Finding a peaceful solution requires two basic things: willingness to think before fighting, and a willingness to communicate for understanding. Try these steps:

* Ask questions, listen, clarify, speak for yourself rather than for the other one (I messages).
* Search for possible solutions, accept all suggestions without initial comment, clarify again.
* Identify and explore those options, looking especially for those that allow everyone to win (or at least not to lose).
* Develop an action plan or make agreements for current and future behavior.
* Agree to trust those decisions. If someone appears to break the trust, use the same cycle to learn the truth.

Teen *mediation* is a practice in which two people or groups agree to have an outside individual or team of peers listen to a grievance. The mediator does not tell anyone what to do, but helps each party through the steps described above. The mediator concentrates on the process to ensure that persons are heard and their positions are understood.

Several other types of problem solving are related. In *negotiation*, both parties work things out together. Each one may give something and get something. *Arbitrators*, third parties, listen to a dispute and make a decision that both sides agree to accept. *Litigation* and *legislation* are more formal or legal means to problem solving, in which a judge decides or a law is passed.

Roleplaying: Nonviolent Responses
(30 minutes)

☞ Select several members of the group to roleplay the four scenarios listed below and/or add others of your own. Review the techniques of teen mediation and nonviolent problem solving methods in the tint box.

☞ Solicit suggestions from the whole group for some nonviolent responses that might be substituted for the violent actions that appear in each situation. Ask for alternate responses from the participants as well as the onlookers.

1. Bret, known as the school bully, throws you up against your locker and threatens to "knock your head off" if you don't let him see your math homework.

2. Janine is in a rotten mood. She is brooding while going to her next class and accidentally bumps into you. She yells at you for not watching where you are going. You yell back, then you both begin exchanging insults until Janine calls you a vulgar name. A friend in the crowd that gathered says to you, "Are you going to let that ___ call you that?"

3. Someone repeated some gossip about a student being pregnant and wrongly attributed it to you. The girl's boyfriend runs with a rough bunch and confronts you with this insult to his girl. He usually carries a weapon.

4. You have a very hot temper. You see Carl steal something from your locker. Should you get him now or wait until Carl is alone? What will you do to him?

Scripture Study and Worship
(30 minutes)

☞ Begin this time together by singing "Let There Be Peace on Earth" (*The United Methodist Hymnal*, No. 431)

☞ Ask someone to read aloud **Matthew 26:47-56**. Begin a discussion of this passage with the following statements and questions:

■ Jesus' response to his arrest was a nonviolent one.

■ Jesus says he could have asked God to send legions of angels to save him. Why do you think he refused to take that course of action?

■ Jesus found himself in a very violent situation. What do you think his example tells us about how God would want us to act when we find ourselves in violent situations?

☞ Have the group members gather in a worshipful setting. Sit in a circle and have someone read aloud **Ephesians 4:1-3, 25-32**.

☞ Instruct the participants to stand up and to put their arms around one another's shoulders. Invite everyone to respond to the following: "If you ever felt like hitting someone, drop your arms. If you ever felt as if there was nothing you could do about violence in your community, take a step back. If you ever bought a record, book, magazine, or watched a movie or TV show with violence in it, take another step back. If you ever felt that media violence doesn't affect you, turn around. If you ever felt that violence was something you should be concerned about as a Christian, turn around. If you ever watched a G-rated movie or read a nonviolent book and enjoyed it, take a step forward. If you ever felt concerned about the violence in your community, take another step forward. If you ever forgave someone, put your arms around the persons next to you."

☞ Close the Scripture study by singing "Sanctuary."

© 1992 by Cokesbury.

Wendy Downing-Birdwell is an ordained elder in the Missouri East Conference of The United Methodist Church. She attended Central Methodist College in Fayette, Missouri, and Perkins School of Theology on the campus of Southern Methodist University in Dallas, Texas. She is currently living in Sikeston, Missouri, and is on leave of absence to stay home with her two small children.

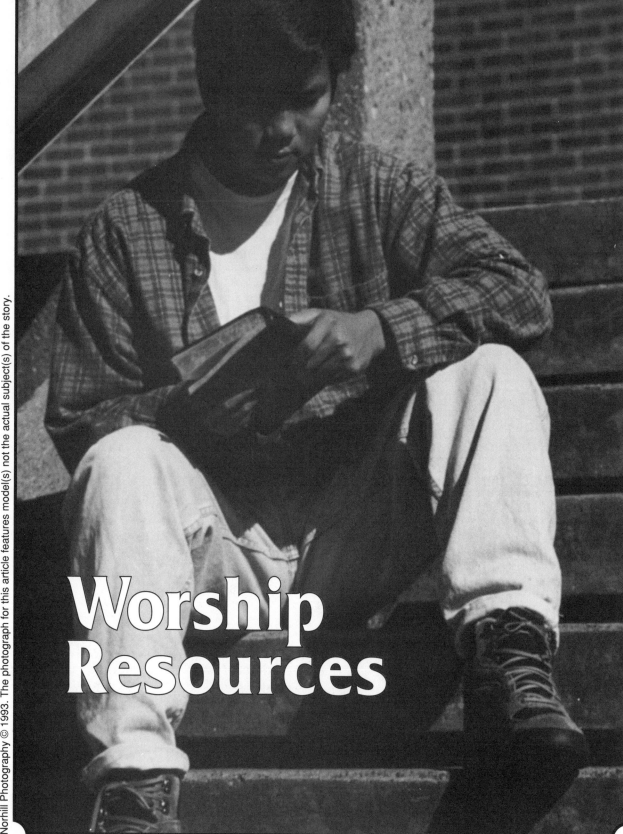

Norhill Photography © 1993. The photograph for this article features model(s) not the actual subject(s) of the story.

Worship Resources

Occasional Prayers

Prayer for Hope

O God of the past, present, and future, we pray for all your children who have no hope. For those whose past is filled with pain and disappointment, we pray for faith and the anticipation of change. For those whose present is filled with anxiety and doubt, we pray for courage and faithful expectation. For those who are mired in despair and have no joy or anticipation of the future, we pray for hope. For all the hopeless, help us be agents of reconciliation and change and witnesses of the promise of a future in Jesus Christ. **Amen.**

A Prayer to Cast Out Fear

Merciful God, whose love casts out fear, hold us in your love and comfort when we are afraid. Show us how to live as disciples in a frightening world and how to work to erase fear from our communities. Give us strength to face what scares us. Help us learn to claim and share the power that casts out fear. In Jesus' name. **Amen.**

Prayer for Help in Crisis

Dear God who cares for all creation, give us courage in times of fear, strength in times of doubt, and focus in times of crisis. Surround us with a sense of your presence so we may rest assured of your love, comfort, and direction. Enable us to arise to the needs of others as well as to ask for the help we need ourselves. Give us peace in the presence of panic and guidance in the face of chaos. We ask in the name of our Deliverer, Jesus Christ. **Amen.**

For Victims

Gracious God, who is wounded by the sin of humankind, we ask you to look deep inside the broken hearts of those who have been violated in body or spirit. Heal them of the pain of betrayal; lift from them any added burden of guilty and shameful feelings; free them from the false shackles of blame; and show them how to use their anger and indignation courageously and constructively. Restore their hope and trust of others and protect them from further harm. We ask in Jesus' name. **Amen.**

For Those Who Suffer Ritual Abuse

Dear God, who gives us our faith and our worship as good gifts, we pray for those who are victimized by unholy acts of ritual or worship. Help us to be worthy witnesses of the abundant life available to the worshipping community. Show us the way to open our hearts and the doors of our church to offer healing, joy, and peace to all. **Amen.**

For Victimizers

O God, who exists alone in the perfect and wise use of power, guide those who would use their power to control or hurt others. Heal the wounds, insecurities, insensitivities, and anger that lead them to attack or inflict others. Fill them with a sense of responsibility and Christ-like respect for themselves and others that they will repent of their abusive ways, set right their wrongs, and learn to live in peace. We ask in the name of the true Lord, Jesus Christ. **Amen.**

For Those Who Witness a Tragedy

Merciful God, who saw your own Son crucified, help us who have witnessed a tragedy to deal with the horror of that traumatic event. Guide us in making meaning of what seems meaningless and direct our rage in constructive channels that address the tragedy. Help us to create a nonviolent and peaceful future in which the pain, injury, or death of persons now will not have been in vain. We pray in the name of the Prince of Peace. **Amen.**

From *The United Methodist Book of Worship*

The United Methodist Publishing House, Nashville, Tennessee, 1992.

From *The Book of Common Prayer* for The Episcopal Church

© Kingsport Press: Kingsport, Tennessee, 1977

From the *Book of Common Worship* for the Presbyterian Church (U.S.A.) and the Cumberland Presbyterian Church

© 1993 Westminster/John Knox Press, Louisville, Kentucky.

From the *Lutheran Book of Worship*

Augsburg Publishing House, Minneapolis, and Board of Publications, Lutheran Church in America, Philadelphia. © 1978.

Where to Go for Help

Where to Go for Help

Help, Support, and Resources

Myths About Child Abuse

▶ Child abuse is limited to certain races or certain socioeconomic groups or certain professions. (Don't assume that the white, well-to-do social worker could not be abusing her children.)

▶ Child abuse is a new phenomenon.

▶ Child abuse is a rare occurrence.

▶ Child abuse in a family occurs to all children, or child abuse cannot be limited to one child in a family.

▶ A child abuser is fairly easy to pick out.

▶ Sexual child abuse has largely to do with sex and sexual drive.

▶ Children victims show overt fear of their abuser.

▶ Time alone heals child abuse wounds.

▶ Nice, polite Christians don't discuss sex.

▶ It is important to keep the family together at all costs.

▶ A child abuser can "repent" and be "cured" without professional help.

▶ Good and bad touching should not be taught or discussed because it causes children to make up stories.

▶ The Christian way to deal with child abuse is to forgive and forget.

Extent of Violence in the Family

Forty-three percent of teenagers say they have experienced some form of physical violence at home. The most common perpetrators of this violence are fathers (54%) and brothers (52%). Other family members involved include mothers (40%), sisters (21%), and other relatives (11%).

Types of violence range from mild forms to extreme forms. Here are the types teenagers experience ranked in order:

▶ Slapping: 33%

▶ Pushing and shoving: 27%

▶ Hitting with fists: 18%

▶ Throwing objects: 16%

▶ Kicking: 16%

▶ Throwing the victim: 12 %

▶ Hitting victim with an object: 11%

▶ Beating: 9%

▶ Biting: 6%

▶ Choking: 6%

▶ Threatening with a knife or gun: 4%

▶ Using a knife or gun: 2%

SOURCE: Study of 204 high school juniors and seniors reported in Bruce Roscoe and John E. Callahan, 'Adolescents' Self-Reporting of Violence in Families and Dating Relations. Adolescence, Fall 1985, pages 545-553.

Steps to Take if You Suspect Child Abuse

If you suspect child abuse, you must learn your state laws that will answer the following questions:

▶ Does civil immunity for reporting extend to everyone who reports, or only those mandated by law to report? Is the teen leader's reporting anonymous? Is the reporter's subsequent testimony at trial also protected?

▶ To whom do you report? law enforcement? to a Social Services/Child Protection Agency? both or either one? Must the report be in writing or will a telephone call suffice?

▶ What triggers a requirement to report? Any "suspicion of abuse"? A "reasonable belief" that the child has been abused? Some "hard evidence" that an abuse has actually been committed?

▶ What is common law? ". . . the body of those principles and rules of action, relating to the government and security of persons and property, which derive their authority solely from usages and customs of immemorial antiquity. . ." *Black's Law Dictionary*, by Henry C. Black, Revised Fourth Edition, West Publishing Co., 1968.

*Do*s and *Don't*s Concerning Child Abuse

Do:

▶ Be familiar with your state's child abuse laws.

▶ Be on the alert for child abuse at all times.

▶ Write down everything a teen says.

▶ Believe the teen and show it.

▶ Offer support.

▶ Be honest about your duty to report.

▶ Show caring and sympathy.

▶ Report the abuse.

▶ Anticipate that the family will not be pleased with your knowledge and position.

Do Not:

▶ Assume that you know the law without yearly review and update.

▶ Believe that you can easily identify an abuse victim or abuser.

▶ Rely on your memory.

▶ Assume abuse does not happen in a "good" family.

▶ Promise to fix everything.

▶ Tell the teen every word is confidential.

▶ Show horror, disgust, alarm.

▶ Try to resolve the situation yourself.

▶ Expect to be "thanked" by anyone, especially the teen's family.

Where to Go for Help if You Suspect Child Abuse

▶ AMACS (Adults Molested as Children)

▶ Daughters and Sons United (sexually abused persons)

▶ Teacher/school counselor

▶ Pastor of church/youth counselor

▶ Medical doctor

▶ Mental health clinic/social worker

▶ Department of Human Services/district attorney

▶ National Child Abuse Hotline—800-422-4453

▶ In most states, professionals who suspect abuse are required by law to report their suspicions to the authorities. One's first concern should be for the victim and to help in any way possible.

Other Sources of Help

Consider contacting one or more of the agencies or persons, listed below, when dealing with violence, abuse, and/or neglect within the family.

▶ Self-help groups such as Alanon (for the family members of alcoholics), Alateen (for teenage alcoholics and teen family members of alcoholics), CODA (Codependents Anonymous), ACOA (Adult Children of Alcoholics), Naranon (Narcotics Anonymous)

▶ Believe the Children Newsletter. PO Box 268462, Chicago, IL 60626. (708) 515-5432.

About Date Rape

▶ Victims of date/acquaintance rape are usually high school or college age youth.

▶ Date/acquaintance rape (forced sex without one's consent) is wrong under all circumstances.

▶ If teenagers of both sexes become aware of how date/acquaintance rape happens, they can start to take steps to protect themselves.

▶ Four out of five teenage rape victims are assaulted by someone they know.

▶ Of these victims, 56 percent are raped on a date.

▶ 30 percent are raped by a friend.

▶ 11 percent are raped by a boyfriend.

▶ 78 percent of rape victims do not tell their parents.

▶ 71 percent of rape victims confide in a friend or friends.

▶ Only 6 percent of date/acquaintance rapes are reported to the police.

▶ Date/acquaintance rape is as traumatic and serious as other types of rape.

▶ Date/acquaintance rape is against the law.

▶ Date/acquaintance rape is not the victim's fault.

▶ Forcing sex on an unwilling partner is never okay.

▶ A person always has the right to (and SHOULD) say no to unwanted sexual activity.

What To Do in the Event of Rape

Rape is a crime of violence that demeans everyone involved. Emotional scars can last far longer than any physical injury. The unfortunate reality is that sometimes saying no and firmly resisting is not enough.

▶ Call the police immediately after a rape occurs. The victim should not change clothes or take a bath, in order to protect physical evidence.

▶ Make sure the survivor's medical needs have been met.

▶ Ask how the survivor is feeling and let him/her know that feelings such as anger, fear, guilt, confusion, and such are normal.

▶ Assure the victim that he/she is not to blame. This is the criminal's responsibility.

▶ Allow the victim to regain some type of control over her situation. Ask permission of the victim to do simple things. May we talk now? Would you like me to call you by your first name? All of these questions provoke decisions which, however small, help the victim reassert control.

▶ Find out the most immediate problem facing the victim in the aftermath of the crime. Help the victim explore options in solving the problem and let him/her decide what will be the best option.

▶ Let the victim know what she or he can anticipate in the future—emotional reactions, the involvement of the criminal justice system, and other concerns that might arise in the aftermath.

▶ Seek the support of family members and contact a community rape and sexual abuse center or a crisis center.

▶ Discuss how friends can help another friend who has been raped, either in a date/acquaintance situation or by a stranger and how to help someone who is afraid to talk to her or his parents.

▶ Discuss any organizations in the local area that welcome youth involvement in rape prevention.

▶ Contact a Crisis Counselling Center in your state or community. May deal with a variety of crises, such as rape, domestic violence, child abuse, and suicide. See your Yellow Pages under Social Services or Human Services.

Read more about Date Rape

Camp Fire Youth Survey (Focus: Date Rape) provided the statistics for the "Attitudes" sidebar. The survey, to gauge teen attitudes toward contemporary issues, was commissioned by Camp Fire Boys and Girls (Kansas City, Missouri) in 1992. For more information, contact Shea Walsworth of Fleishman-Hillard Research at 816-474-9407.

Dimensions: Women's Place, Men's Place, Our Place (for youth and group leaders), by Janet Comperry Lowdermilk (Friendship Press, 1992).

"Standing Up to Peer Pressure," by Nan Duerling, Stand Your Ground: Christian Youth Under Pressure (leader's guide and student leaflets; Cokesbury, 1991).

▶ Contact the Center for the Prevention of Sexual and Domestic Violence, 1914 North 34th St., Suite 105, Seattle, WA 98103-9058. 206-634-1903

Violence in Our Streets

Chances that an American boy or man will be a homicide victim

AGE	WHITE	AFRICAN AMERICAN
at birth	1 in 205	1 in 27
at 20	1 in 232	1 in 31
at 40	1 in 525	1 in 83

From 1989 statistics from the FBI's Uniform Crime Reports as reprinted in USA TODAY WEEKEND October 2-4, 1992, "Can TV Help Save Black Youth?" by Diane Goldner.

Firearms Kept in Homes

65% in Southern homes
42% in Midwest homes
41% in Northeast homes
39% in Western homes

Reported in *New York Times*, April 3, 1992

Regional Homicide Rate

12 per 100,000 in South
7 per 100,000 in Midwest
9 per 100,000 in Northeast
9 per 100,000 in West

From Uniform Crime Reports 1990: Crime in the United States

▶ The Department of Health and Human Services reports that gunshot wounds now are responsible for more deaths among all male teenagers, both black and white than all natural causes combined. Reported in the *Washington Post,* March 14, 1991.

Eye Opening Numbers

The following is from *Media&Values* No. 62, The Center for Media and Values, 1962 Shenandoah St., Los Angeles, CA 90034

▶ By the age of 16, the average child spends as much time watching TV as in school.

▶ The average child is reported to log roughly 36,000 hours of television by the time he or she is 18, viewing some 15,000 murders.

▶ In 1992 the US Surgeon General cited violence as the leading cause of injury to women ages 15 to 44, and the US Center for Disease Control considers violence a leading public health issue, to be treated as an epidemic.

▶ A report issued by the National Institute of Mental Health (covering 10 years of research) stated 'the concensus among most of the research community is that violence on television does lead to aggressive behavior by children and teenagers who watch the programs.'

More Numbers

▶ In 1990, guns were used to kill 6,795 teenagers and young adults under the age of 25. This does not include the youth who use guns to commit suicide.

▶ The National Center for Health Statictics says that, since 1988, teenage boys in the United States are more likely to die from gunshot wounds than from all natural causes combined.

▶ Homicide is the leading cause of death among Black youth, ages 18-24. The Centers for Disease Control reports that from 1984-1988, the murder rate among Black youth, ages 15-19 rose 100 percent.

▶ During a six month period in 1988-89, more than 400,000 students were victims of violent crime at school.

▶ A 1990 survey of students in 31 Illinois schools showed that one in 20 carried guns to school.

▶ Arrests for the murder of boys 12-years-old and under doubled between 1985 and 1991.

▶ The United states spends at least one billion dollars a year on hospital care for persons who have been shot and who frequently have no health insurance.

Source: The Children's Defense Fund

Number of people murdered by handguns in 1990, by country:

Australia	10
Sweden	13
Great Britain	22
Canada	68
Switzerland	91
Japan	87
United States	10,567

Source: The Children's Defense Fund

Signs and Symptoms of Ritualistic Abuse in Children

▶ Child touches others sexually, asks for sex, interacts in an inappropriately sexualized fashion. Child is sexually provocative or seductive.

▶ Child shows age-inappropriate sexual knowledge.

▶ Child fears attending church, becomes agitated or upset in church, fears religious objects or people, refuses to worship God.

▶ Child may experience eating problems, for example: binging, gorging, refusing to eat.

▶ Child may suffer from emotional problems such as mood swings, displaying anxious behavior, can't sleep, troubling frequent nightmares.

▶ Child may exhibit problems in peer relations.

Who to Contact for Support and Help for Ritual Abuse

For additional information about ritual abuse write: **International Cult Education Program**, P.O. Box 1232, Gracie Station, New York, NY 10028, 212-439-1550.

Center for the Treatment of Ritualistic Deviance, Hart Grove Hospital, 520 North Ridgewal Ave., Chicago, IL 60624 312-722-3113.

Read more about Gangs, Hate Crimes

When Hate Groups Come To Town, A Handbook of Effective Community Responses © 1992, Center for Democratic Renewal and Education, Inc. P.O. Box 50469, Atlanta, GA 30302-0469. 404-221-0025

Dreams Under Fire. (© 1992 Franciscan Communications) VHS, color, 50 minutes. A documentary that looks at the causes and consequences of gangs in two different environments. Available from TeleKETIC Productions, Franciscan Communications, 1229 S. Santee Street, Los Angeles, California 90015-2566.

Christianity, Patriarchy, and Abuse: A Feminist Critique, by Joanne Carlson Brown and Carole R. Bohn (New York: Pilgrim Press, 1989)

Texts of Terror: Literary-Feminist Readings of Biblical Narratives, by Phyllis Trible (Philadelphia: Fortress Press, 1984)

The Bible, Violence, and the Sacred: Liberation from the Myth of Sanctioned Violence, by James G. Williams (New York: HarperCollins, 1991)

Youth Advocacy—Step by Step. 659 Big Ugly Creek Rd. East, Leet, WV 25536. 304-855-8557.

Shalom Zones Program (General Board of Church and Society) 100 Maryland Ave., NE, Washington, DC 20002-5664. 202-488-5600

Violence Prevention Curriculum for Adolescents by Deborah Prothrow-Stith. EDC Publishing Center, Educational Development Center, 55 Chapel St. Suite 24, Newton, MA 02160

Carnegie Quarterly—Volume XXXVII/Number 4, Fall 1992. "Adolescent Health: A Generation At Risk". 437 Madison Avenue, New York, NY 10022. 212-371-3200.

Read More on
Violence and What You Can Do About It

Media&Values Magazine, 1962 South Shenandoah St., Los Angeles, CA 90034.

Deadly Consequences: How Violence is Destroying Our Teenage Population and a Plan to Begin Solving the Problem, by Deborah Prothrow-Stith and Michaele Weissman, published 1991 by Harper-Collins publishers, 10 East 53rd St., New York, NY 10022.

Words That Hurt Words That Heal: Language About God and People. A churchwide study from the 1988 General Conference of The United Methodist Church. Available from Cokesbury, FF3-147130. $2.00. 800-672-1789

Language of Hospitality: Intercultural Relations in the Household of God. A guidebook that helps senior high youth and adults learn how to practice cultural inclusiveness through language and actions. Available from Cokesbury, FFD-757762. $3.50. 800-672-1789

Creating a New Community: God's People Overcoming Racism. This resource provides a Christian perspective on issues related to racism in the church and community and examines ways to change discriminatory policies and practices. Available from Cokesbury, FF3-754321. $2.25. 800-672-1789

Challenge: Christian Perpsectives on Social Issues, Volume 3 Violence. This resource examines both the Bible and violence; Christians and self-defense; American culture and the right to bear arms; an issue pertaining to global peace. Available from Cokesbury, FF3-782082. $3.95. 800-672-1789

Challenge, Volume 1 Faith for Life. Explores John Wesley's understanding of personal faith and social action, the implications of Christian faith for one's choice and practice of vocation, the rural crisis in the US, and the search for peace and justice in Central America. FF3-752310. $3.95. 800-672-1789

Challenge, Volume 2 Life and Death. Studies the biblical understanding of death, reflects on the concern for dignity in the face of terminal illness, considers the complex of issues involved in thinking about abortion, and examines the moral and legal dimensions of capital punishment. FF3-752426. $3.95. 800-672-1789

Revival of Hope: Youth Making a Difference. Show concerned youth ways to make a difference where they are—Middle school/Junior high and Senior high—with skill development through contemporary and Bible stories. *Revival of Hope* helps youth: assess their need and resources, be aware of issues and possibilities, and act on what is possible. Available from Cokesbury, Youth Kit FF3-759390. $49.95. 800-672-1789

Building a New Community: God's Children Overcoming Racism. This resource empowers middle schoolers to deal with racism and work toward the vision of acceptance of all people. Available from Cokesbury. FF3-757789. $8.95 800-672-1789

On Line with Jesus Christ. This resource teaches life skills of communication, decision making, goal setting, and building positive relationships as part of being an active follower of Jesus Christ. Available from Cokesbury.FF3-475457. $170.00 800-672-1789

Contact the Institute for American Pluralism. The American Jewish Committee, 55 East Jackson Boulevard, Suite 1880, Chicago, IL 60604. 312-663-5400.

Christian Social Action (Magazine) June 1993. Special Issue on Youth and Violence, 100 Maryland Ave., NE, Washington DC 20002. 202-488-5621.

Search Institute Catalogs. Practical research benefiting children and youth. 700 South Third St., Suite 210, Minneapolis, MN 55415. 800-888-7828.